Chronicle
of the year 1996

A DORLING KINDERSLEY BOOK

Chronicle of the year 96
Written, edited, and designed by
GLS Editorial and Design
Garden Studios, 11–15 Betterton Street,
London WC2H 9BP

GLS EDITORIAL AND DESIGN

Project editor Victoria Sorzano
Design director Ruth Shane
Editorial directors Reg Grant, Jane Laing

Author Reg Grant
Contributors Victoria Sorzano, Adrian Gilbert, Jane Laing

Picture research David Towersey, Frances Vargo
Index Kay Ollerenshaw

DORLING KINDERSLEY

Project editor Annabel Morgan
Production manager Ian Paton
Managing art editor Derek Coombes
Managing editor Frank Ritter

First published in Great Britain in 1997
by Dorling Kindersley Limited
9 Henrietta Street, London WC2E 8PS

A CIP catalogue record for this book is available from the British Library
ISBN 0-7513-3017-5

Reproduced by Kestrel Digital Colour Ltd., Chelmsford, Essex
Printed and bound in Great Britain by Butler & Tanner

Chronicle
of the year 1996

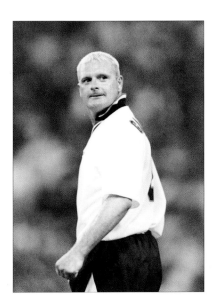

DK

DORLING KINDERSLEY

LONDON • NEW YORK • STUTTGART • MOSCOW

January

S	M	T	W	T	F	S
	1	2	3	4	5	6
7	8	9	10	11	12	13
14	15	16	17	18	19	20
21	22	23	24	25	26	27
28	29	30	31			

Lurgan, County Armagh, 1
Ian Lyons, 31, is shot dead by gunmen. A group called Direct Action Against Drugs, believed to be a front for the IRA, admits responsibility.

London, 2
Salman Rushdie wins the Whitbread Book of the Year award for his novel *The Moor's Last Sigh*.

London, 3
A deportation order is brought against Saudi dissident Mohammed al-Mas'ari. He is to be expelled from the UK to the island of Dominica in the Caribbean.

Cape Town, 4
England's cricketers lose the fifth Test and the series to South Africa.

Washington, DC, 4
The Congressional panel investigating the firing of White House travel-office staff in 1993 reveals an administrative memo linking Hillary Clinton to the dismissals.

Camden, London, 4
A 15-year-old boy is charged with the murder of headmaster Philip Lawrence last month. (→ October 17)

Norwich, 4
A report from the University of East Anglia says that last year was the hottest ever recorded, apparent confirmation of global warming.

City of London, 4
The London Stock Exchange fires its chief executive Michael Lawrence in a vote of no confidence.

Washington, DC, 5
The US Congress votes funds to return government employees to work, after a partial shutdown caused by the failure of President Clinton and Congress to agree a budget.

Tokyo, 5
Japanese prime minister Tomiichi Murayama announces he is to resign. (→ January 11)

Washington, DC, 5
Hillary Clinton's billing records from the Rose Law Firm, crucial evidence in the Whitewater affair, are released by the White House, having turned up inexplicably after being missing for two years. (→ January 22)

BOSNIA, TUESDAY 2

US troops pour into Bosnia

US troops make their way across the pontoon bridge from Croatia into Bosnia.

US ground forces are taking up their positions in northeastern Bosnia today, as the NATO peacekeeping mission begins in earnest.

On Sunday US Army engineers finally completed a 600-m (650-yd) pontoon bridge over the Sava River, which divides Bosnia from Croatia. As soon as it was finished units of the First Cavalry Brigade, First Armored Division began riding across from Zupanja on the Croatian side to Orasje in Bosnia.

Eventually 20,000 US troops will occupy the Posavina corridor that separates Serb and Muslim Bosnian territory, to help enforce the peace agreement negotiated in Dayton, Ohio, last November. (→ January 13)

LONDON, FRIDAY 5

Clandestine video shows pregnant Holloway prisoner in chains

Home Office minister Anne Widdecombe has defended the shackling of pregnant prisoners in labour, claiming it prevents escape attempts. "But we have an absolute rule that we don't handcuff women or restrain them while they are actually in childbirth," the minister said.

The practice was brought to light by a clandestine film shown on Channel 4. It showed a pregnant Holloway prison inmate chained to a bed while in labour. The woman was again chained and handcuffed immediately after the birth. (→ January 15)

Home Office minister Anne Widdecombe says the restraining practice is justified.

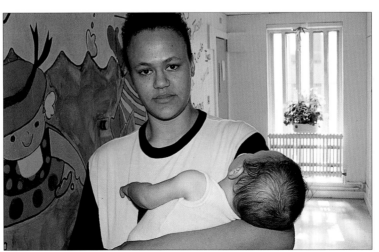

A new mother at Holloway prison: Inmates in labour wards are usually kept shackled.

BRISTOL, MONDAY 1

Local hero shot dead by armed muggers

One man was killed and two others injured when they intervened to stop an armed robbery in the St. Paul's district of Bristol this morning. The dead man was Evon "Bangy" Berry, a father of three. Police say Mr. Berry was killed by a single shot to the head. The four muggers fled by car.

Mr. Berry was a caretaker at a local community centre. His widow described him as "a big, gentle person who would not hurt anyone".

STRATHCLYDE, TUESDAY 2

Thaw brings water shortages to the north

The New Year's big thaw has brought only misery to hundreds of thousands of customers of the water companies. Across large areas of Scotland and the north of England leaks from burst water mains have either reduced or completely cut off water supplies.

In Strathclyde, the worst affected area, 500,000 people are without running water. Residents queued with buckets for water from tankers.

Hamas bomber killed by booby trap

Yahya Ayyash, known as "the Engineer", was the mastermind behind many of the terrorist bombings that Israel has suffered in the last two years. Today he is dead, himself a victim of a murderous explosion. Ayyash was killed by a small but deadly explosive charge packed into a mobile phone believed to have been prepared by the Israeli secret service.

Ayyash, 32, was a member of Hamas, the extremist Islamic group. His death took place in the Gaza Strip, now under the control of Yassir Arafat's PLO. A Hamas militant warned: "The Hamas brigades will reach the hand behind this crime and will deal with it as it should be dealt with." (→ February 25)

At the funeral of murdered Hamas explosives expert Yahya Ayyash (above left), the coffin is mobbed by thousands of supporters.

Los Angeles, Wednesday 3. Pop star Madonna testified in court today against stalker Robert Dewey Hoskins. Hoskins allegedly twice entered the grounds of Madonna's home, said he intended to marry her, and threatened to cut her throat "from ear to ear". (→ January 8)

Ailing Saudi ruler hands control to his brother

King Fahd of Saudi Arabia has handed over the management of government affairs to his half-brother, Prince Abdullah. King Fahd is 74 years old and suffered a severe stroke last November.

The stability of Saudi Arabia, the world's largest oil exporter, is of vital importance to Western powers. The Saudis have repeatedly upheld Western interests in the Middle East, most notably during the Desert Storm operation against Iraq in 1991. Prince Abdullah is thought to favour a less pro-US policy than the king. (→ February 21)

Saudi leaders: Prince Abdullah (left) and his half-brother King Fahd (waving).

Hunt continues for the murderer of student Celine Figard

The detective leading the investigation into the murder of French student Celine Figard has rejected speculation that a serial killer might be responsible for her death.

John McCammont, chief superintendent of West Mercia CID, said the police still wanted to interview the driver of a white Mercedes lorry who gave Miss Figard a lift at Chieveley service station in Berkshire on December 19 – the last time she was seen alive. Her body was found ten days later in a layby near Worcester. Mr. McCammont said that it would be "an incredible coincidence" if the driver of the lorry Miss Figard had approached just happened to be a serial killer. (→ February 21)

French student Celine Figard, aged 19, killed on her way to visit her cousin.

Physicists announce the creation of antimatter

A team of European physicists has created the first complete atoms of antimatter ever to exist. The 11 atoms of antihydrogen were made at the European Laboratory for Particle Physics, known as CERN, in Geneva last September. The anti-atoms existed for only billionths of a second before being wiped out by collisions with ordinary atoms.

Antimatter is opposite to matter in all its characteristics – with a negative electric charge where matter has a positive one, for example. A practical use for antimatter seems remote, but the history of nuclear physics suggests that it should not be ruled out.

S	M	T	W	T	F	S
	1	2	3	4	5	6
7	8	9	10	11	12	13
14	15	16	17	18	19	20
21	22	23	24	25	26	27
28	29	30	31			

Washington, DC, 8
In the eastern US, from Virginia to Massachusetts, life is brought to a standstill by the heaviest snowfall in more than 70 years.

Singapore, 8
Speaking in the Far East, Labour leader Tony Blair describes his vision of a "stakeholder" society.

Los Angeles, 8
Robert Dewey Hoskins is found guilty of stalking Madonna and assaulting her bodyguard.

Leeds, 8
A Leeds industrial tribunal rules that a Labour party policy forcing some constituencies to choose women candidates contravenes the Sex Discrimination Act.

London, 9
Sir Christopher Bland takes over from Marmaduke Hussey as chairman of the BBC.

Bosnia, 9
A rocket-propelled grenade hits a tram in Sarajevo, killing one civilian.

Irian Jaya, Indonesia, 10
Four Britons are among seven people reportedly taken hostage by tribal rebels in the Indonesian province of Irian Jaya. (→ May 16)

Tokyo, 11
Ryutaru Hashimoto is sworn in as prime minister of Japan.

Rome, 11
Lamberto Dini resigns as Italian prime minister.

Yorkshire, 13
Children queue for anti-meningitis vaccine in South Yorkshire and Nottinghamshire after eight cases of meningitis are found in a month.

London, 13
Miners' leader Arthur Scargill announces he is quitting Labour to set up his own Socialist Labour party. (→ February 1)

Deaths
January 7. Karoly Grosz, former reformist communist leader of Hungary, aged 65.

January 8. François Mitterrand, former president of France, aged 79.

PERVOMAYSKAYA, DAGESTAN, THURSDAY 11

Chechen "Lone Wolf" defies the Russian Bear

Chechen rebels are trapped by Russian forces at the border village of Pervomayskaya.

A band of Chechen separatists and their hostages have been encircled by Russian forces in a small village in Dagestan, close to the Chechen border. The band's leader Salman Raduyev, known as the "Lone Wolf", is demanding free passage to the safety of the Chechen mountains.

On Tuesday the separatists, who are demanding independence for Chechenia, seized a hospital in the Dagestani town of Kizlyar, taking 200 hostages. They were allowed to set out for Chechenia in a convoy of buses but were attacked by Russian forces before reaching the border.

The separatists have taken over the village of Pervomayskaya and are awaiting a Russian attack as helicopters hover overhead. Raduyev has promised that he and his men will die rather than surrender. (→ January 18)

NEWBURY, THURSDAY 11

Bypass protestors take to the trees

Bypass protestors want trees not roads.

A motley collection of environmental and anti-road protestors is mobilizing to block the building of a bypass around the Berkshire town of Newbury. The new road will pass through some of the most beautiful, environmentally sensitive countryside in England, but will also relieve the town of severe traffic congestion.

The stand-off began on Tuesday when protestors prevented work on the project from beginning. Today crews began felling trees but protestors took to the branches to obstruct further work. They were soon constructing aerial walkways and tree houses. Meanwhile the police have begun to make arrests under the new Criminal Justice Act. (→ February 11)

Protestors build tree-top houses and aerial walkways, and encamp in the trees themselves.

JARNAC, FRANCE, THURSDAY 11

Mitterrand is mourned by wife and mistress

Mitterrand's final journey is through the streets of his birthplace, Jarnac. He is laid to rest in the family plot in the town's cemetery.

France's former president, François Mitterrand, who died on Monday, today returned to his birthplace. One of Europe's foremost post-war leaders, he was laid to rest in a sombre family vault in the small town of Jarnac in southwest France. The ceremony was attended by 500 of his friends and associates. His wife Danielle stood alongside his mistress Anne Pingeot and their daughter Mazarine Pingeot.

In Paris, M. Mitterrand's passing was commemorated with greater pomp. Over 2,000 people, including heads of state and political leaders from around the world, attended a solemn requiem mass in Notre-Dame cathedral. The UK was represented by Prince Charles.

M. Mitterrand, who was 79 years old, died of prostate cancer. He had been president from 1981 to 1995.

CITY OF LONDON, THURSDAY 11

Thatcher throws down the gauntlet to pro-Euro Tories

Lady Thatcher trenchantly defended the policies she pursued when she was prime minister in a speech tonight, and implicitly criticized deviations from Thatcherism under her successor, John Major.

Delivering the Keith Joseph Memorial Lecture in the City of London, Lady Thatcher explicitly attacked Tory moderates and pro-Europeans. "I am not sure what is meant by those who say that the party should return to something called One Nation Conservatism," she said. "As far as I can tell by their views on European federalism, such people's creed would be better described as No Nation Conservatism."

LONDON, WEDNESDAY 10

Venables to quit as England coach

England manager Terry Venables.

England football manager Terry Venables announced today that he will not seek to renew his contract after the summer's European Championships.

Venables cited his legal dispute with Tottenham chairman Alan Sugar as the reason for his decision. An FA statement said: "Terry Venables faces a number of time-consuming legal battles in the latter part of 1996 which he believes could interfere with England's efforts to qualify for the final stages of the next World Cup."

Tuzla, Bosnia, Saturday 13. President Clinton, wearing a NATO beret, drops in on the US troops policing the Bosnian ceasefire. Bad weather delayed the president's flight into Tuzla and his stopover there was cut down to three hours.

ENGLAND, THURSDAY 11

Hell is not eternal torment

The doctrine commission of the Church of England has rejected the "sadistical" notion of hell as a place of eternal damnation. According to a commission report published today entitled "The Mystery of Salvation", the idea of hellfire was one of the "appalling theologies which made God into a monster". Hell does exist, the report says, but only as an individual choice of "total non-being". The report is an attempt to reintroduce the understandings of the early church.

Mexico City, Sunday 7. Keiko, the whale who starred in the film *Free Willy*, was flown from an amusement park in Mexico City to an aquarium in Newport, Oregon, today. He may be released into the ocean.

January

S	M	T	W	T	F	S
	1	2	3	4	5	6
7	8	9	10	11	12	13
14	15	16	17	18	19	20
21	22	23	24	25	26	27
28	29	30	31			

Lisbon, 14
Socialist Jorge Sampaio wins national election to succeed Mario Soares as president of Portugal.

Thailand, 14
A Buddhist monk confesses to the murder of British backpacker Johanne Masheder, who had been missing since last December. (→ January 31)

London, 15
The Prison Service announces that the practice of shackling pregnant women is to be dropped.

Mexico City, 15
Top Mexican drug trafficker Juan Garcia Abrego is arrested by Mexican police. He is one of the FBI's ten most-wanted fugitives.

Athens, 15
Andreas Papandreou resigns as Greek prime minister. He is succeeded by Costas Simitis.

Moscow, 16
Anatoli Chubais, the leading economic reformer in the Russian government, resigns as deputy prime minister after differences with President Boris Yeltsin. (→ January 29)

Belfast, 16
Convicted IRA bomber Donna Maguire is awarded £13,500 compensation for twisting her ankle on a loose paving stone.

Milan, 17
Silvio Berlusconi, Italian media tycoon and former prime minister, goes on trial for corruption.

Oslo, 17
Four men are jailed for stealing Edvard Munch's masterpiece, *The Scream*, in February 1994.

Istanbul, 19
The four Chechen gunmen who had hijacked a ferry on the Black Sea surrender to the Turkish authorities.

Deaths
January 15. Moshoeshoe II, king of the southern African state of Lesotho.

January 18. Rudolph Wanderone Jr., known as Minnesota Fats, legendary pool hustler, in Nashville, Tennessee, aged 83.

Maxwells found not guilty of fraud

Ian and Kevin Maxwell, sons of the publishing mogul Robert Maxwell, were cleared of fraud charges at the Old Bailey today. The jury reached its unanimous verdict after 11 days of deliberations.

The brothers had been accused of conspiring to defraud Mirror Group pension funds. The funds' deficit of £440 million emerged after Robert Maxwell's death in November 1991.

The trial lasted 131 days and is estimated to have cost taxpayers over £25 million. The brothers may face further fraud charges in connection with their father's business empire. (→ January 26)

Kevin Maxwell (centre left) and brother Ian (centre right) after their acquittal on Friday.

Modern Lady Godiva shocks Coventry

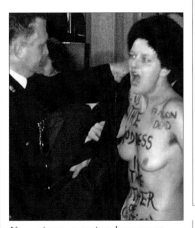

Koyunti protests against the motor car.

A thousand people assembled in Coventry cathedral today for a service to celebrate the centenary of the motor car. Anti-car demonstrators picketed the cathedral and one female protestor brought the service to a halt in a striking manner.

Angel Koyunti, 35, took off her coat in front of the congregation to reveal her naked body scrawled with slogans. "In the spirit of Lady Godiva, I'm here to mourn the death of my mother and the 17 million people killed directly by the motor car," she said.

Ms. Koyunti was cautioned by police and released. She later said: "My naked body is the last resort in trying to get my views across to people."

Space Shuttle Endeavour, Monday 15. Astronaut Daniel Barry works in the space shuttle's cargo bay during the first of two extravehicular activities scheduled during the current space mission.

Queen says she will not pay the Duchess of York's debts

Apparently exasperated by the lavish spending of the Duchess of York, the Queen is refusing to provide any extra cash to bail her out of debts that some believe to be as high as £3 million.

"The Queen has already made generous provisions to the Duchess of York," a spokeswoman said. "It is up to the duchess and her financial advisers to find a solution and it's not a matter for the Queen." Since her separation from Prince Andrew, the Duchess is reckoned to have had an income of about £300,000 a year, but outgoings in excess of £500,000. (→ April 17)

The Duchess of York faces high debts.

DAGESTAN, THURSDAY 18

Chechen rebels and hostages slaughtered

George Burns, comedy legend, is 100 years old

More than 150 Chechen rebels were reported to have been killed by Russian forces as the siege of the village of Pervomayskaya, Dagestan, came to an end. But more than 100 Chechens, including their leader "Lone Wolf" Salman Raduyev, appear to have escaped. It is also feared that many of the bodies found in the village may be those of hostages. The Chechens were holding about 100 hostages when they were trapped by the Russians last week.

Russian president Boris Yeltsin has declared the crisis over and claimed a victory over the rebels. But the Russian media have been heavily critical of the inefficiency of military operations. Efforts by Russian elite troops to take the village were a farcical failure. Soldiers complained of poor leadership and lack of support. Twenty-six Russian soldiers are reported killed in the fighting and 93 others wounded. On

Chechen gunman with ferry hostages.

Wednesday the Russians resorted to pounding Pervomayskaya with indiscriminate Grad rocket fire, reducing the village to ruins.

In a separate incident on Tuesday, Chechen gunmen hijacked a ferry in the Black Sea and forced it to sail from Trabzon in Turkey towards the Bosphorus. About 200 passengers, mostly Russians, are being held hostage. The gunmen are demanding an end to the siege of Pervomayskaya. They may end the hijacking now that their demands no longer apply.

Russia enjoys the full support of the US administration for its use of military force to counter hostage taking and acts of terrorism by the Chechen rebels. (→ January 19)

Pervomayskaya after the Russian attack; some of the bodies may be those of hostages.

A Chechen commando tries to negotiate with Russian forces during the siege.

US comedian George Burns.

One of America's best loved comedians, George Burns, is 100 years old today. Burns had planned to put on a show at Las Vegas for his centenary birthday. Tickets for the event were already sold when a fall in a bath in July 1994 made him too frail.

Born in New York as Nathan Birnbaum, Burns married Gracie Allen in 1925. The *George Burns and Gracie Allen Show* was a fixture of 1950s' TV. Gracie has been dead for more than 20 years, but George is still making wisecracks and still smoking the cigars – El Producto Queens – that became his trademark. (→ March 9)

Los Angeles, Thursday 18. Lisa Marie Presley has filed for divorce from singer Michael Jackson. The couple have been married for 15 months.

S	M	T	W	T	F	S
	1	2	3	4	5	6
7	8	9	10	11	12	13
14	15	16	17	18	19	20
21	22	23	24	25	26	27
28	29	30	31			

Washington, DC, 22
Hillary Clinton is subpoenaed to testify before a grand jury investigating the mysterious reappearance of her legal billing records connected to the Whitewater affair. (→ January 26)

City of London, 23
Granada wins control of the Forte hotel chain. The hostile takeover cost Granada an estimated £3.9 billion.

Netherlands, 23
The Dutch aircraft manufacturer Fokker, facing bankruptcy, files for protection from its creditors.

Warsaw, 24
Polish prime minister Jozef Oleksy resigns after allegations that he worked as a spy for Russia.

London, 25
An inquest returns a verdict of unlawful killing in the case of Nigerian asylum-seeker Shiji Lapite, who died after a struggle with two police officers in December 1994.

London, 25
The Prince of Wales claims that the planned celebrations for the millennium lack a spiritual dimension, focusing on the "merely material".

London, 26
The Serious Fraud Office announces it is to launch a second prosecution over the collapse of the Maxwell publishing empire. One of the accused will be Kevin Maxwell, cleared in the first prosecution. (→ September 19)

Washington, DC, 26
Hillary Clinton testifies before a grand jury. She emerges apparently confident that her name is cleared. (→ June 18)

Utah, 26
Child murderer John Albert Taylor is executed by firing squad in Utah state prison.

Britain, 27
Fifty football matches are cancelled as Britain is blanketed with snow from Scotland to as far south as Essex. Temperatures drop to a low of -17°C (-1°F).

Deaths
January 23. Norman MacCaig, Scottish poet, aged 85.

WESTMINSTER, THURSDAY 25

Harman chooses grammar school for her child

Labour's shadow health secretary Harriet Harman has caused a political storm by deciding to send her 11-year-old son Joe to a selective grammar school: St. Olave's in Orpington, Kent. Labour's education policy is opposed to selection.

The Conservatives are accusing Harman of hypocrisy, and some Labour politicians have demanded her resignation. But she has the support of Labour leader Tony Blair, who accused the Tories of "trying to turn the education of an 11-year-old child into a political football".

Harman claims that she opposes selection, but that she has made the right choice for her child. "That is what parents do," she said.

Labour's Harriet Harman: Maintains she has made the right choice for her child.

WASHINGTON, DC, TUESDAY 23

Clinton wins applause

President Clinton's State of the Union address gets a warm reception from Congress.

Delivering his State of the Union address to Congress this evening, President Bill Clinton staked his claim to the centre ground in American politics. Borrowing from many Republican themes, he promised measures to promote family life and crack down on crime, declaring that, "the era of big government is over". Most observers agree that the president radiated confidence, buoyed up by a high standing in opinion polls.

Congress also gave a standing ovation to Hillary Clinton, described by the president as "a wonderful wife, a magnificent mother, and a great first lady". She faces a grand jury hearing later in the week. (→ January 26)

Los Angeles, Sunday 21. Nicolas Cage (above left), star of *Leaving Las Vegas*, tonight won the Golden Globe award for best actor in a drama. Emma Thompson's movie *Sense and Sensibility* (above right) took awards for best drama and best screenplay. Other winners included Jimmy Smits of *NYPD Blue* for best TV actor and Nicole Kidman for best movie comedy actress.

JERUSALEM, SUNDAY 21

Arafat triumphs in first Palestinian elections

Yassir Arafat participates in Gaza airport's inauguration ceremony the day before Palestinians turn out to vote.

Yassir Arafat and his Fatah movement have triumphed in elections that could be a major step towards Palestinian statehood. Palestinians in the West Bank, Gaza, and East Jerusalem voted yesterday to elect a president and a legislative council to run the Palestinian autonomous areas, granted self-rule by Israel as part of the Middle East peace process.

Standing for president, Arafat won around 88 per cent of the votes cast. Fatah candidates took 50 seats in the 88-seat Palestinian council. An exultant Arafat declared: "This is a new era. This is the foundation of our Palestinian state."

The militant Islamic movement Hamas, which rejects the peace process, called on voters to boycott the elections, but this was widely ignored. International observers were worried by cases of intimidation during the campaign. But they agreed that the vote could "reasonably be regarded as an accurate expression of the will of the voters on polling day". (→ February 12)

BELFAST, WEDNESDAY 24

US envoy backs IRA on weapons issue

An international commission headed by US senator George Mitchell has advised that paramilitary groups in Northern Ireland should not be obliged to begin disarming before peace negotiations begin.

The British government and the IRA have been deadlocked over the continuing British demand for the decommissioning of weapons as a pre-condition for peace talks. Senator Mitchell stated that the laying down of arms by the paramilitaries should proceed in parallel with peace negotiations, and should be under independent supervision.

Prime Minister John Major responded to the report by calling for elections to an all-party forum that would negotiate a permanent settlement. Sinn Fein, the political wing of the IRA, reacted angrily to the proposal for elections, which are favoured by Ulster Unionists. (→ February 10)

KAHRAMANMARAS, TURKEY, THURSDAY 25

Essex girl's Turkish marriage

At the centre of a storm: 13-year-old Sarah Cook and 18-year-old Musa Komeagac.

Sarah Cook, a 13-year-old girl from Braintree, Essex, has become the focus of an international controversy after going through a Muslim marriage ceremony with an 18-year-old Turkish waiter.

Sarah met the young waiter, Musa Komeagac, last summer on a family holiday in Alanya on the south coast of Turkey. She returned to Turkey to marry him, with the full approval of her parents.

The romance turned sour when the authorities in both Britain and Turkey became aware of the marriage. On Tuesday Sarah's "husband" was arrested and charged with rape in a Turkish court. Under Turkish law a Muslim marriage ceremony has no validity if not accompanied by a civil ceremony, and the minimum age for a legal marriage is 14.

On Wednesday, in Britain, Sarah was made a ward of court at the instigation of Essex County Council, and was ordered to return to Britain. She is living with Komeagac's family in the Turkish town of Kahramanmaras. In a GMTV interview her father said: "We just went along with her dreams. But now her dreams have been shattered by the Turkish government."

Sarah, who now wears a Muslim headscarf, wishes to stay in Turkey. She told reporters: "I used to think I was an ugly girl when I was in Britain. Now I feel I'm beautiful because I'm being loved." (→ February 6)

Paris, Sunday 21. British fashion designer John Galliano, the son of a south London plumber, presents his first *haute couture* collection for Parisian fashion house Givenchy. Naomi Campbell was among the supermodels on the catwalk.

January

S	M	T	W	T	F	S
	1	2	3	4	5	6
7	8	9	10	11	12	13
14	15	16	17	18	19	20
21	22	23	24	25	26	27
28	29	30	31			

Johannesburg, 28
Nation of Islam leader Louis Farrakhan meets with South African president Nelson Mandela.

Canberra, 28
Australian prime minister Paul Keating calls parliamentary elections for March 2. (→ March 3)

Melbourne, 28
In the Australian Open tennis championships, Boris Becker defeats Michael Chang to win the men's singles, and Monica Seles wins the women's title, defeating Anke Huber.

Niamey, Niger, 28
An army coup in the francophone West African state of Niger brings the armed forces chief of staff, Colonel Ibrahim Bare Mainassara, to power.

Paris, 29
French president Jacques Chirac announces an end to the French underground nuclear-test programme that had provoked worldwide protests.

Montreal, 29
The francophone separatist leader Lucien Bouchard is sworn in as premier of Quebec.

Johannesburg, 29
Eight people are killed and 23 are wounded when gunmen open fire on a queue of jobseekers outside a factory.

Bangkok, 31
The Thai monk convicted of killing British backpacker Johanne Masheder is sentenced to death by firing squad.

City of London, 31
The Hanson Group conglomerate announces that it is to split up in an £11 billion demerger.

Athens, 31
Greece backs down from a military confrontation with Turkey over the disputed owernership of the island of Imia in the Aegean.

Deaths
January 28. Jerry Siegel, one of the creators of *Superman*, in Los Angeles, aged 81.

January 29. Joseph Brodsky, Russian-born writer, in New York, aged 55.

PENNSYLVANIA, SUNDAY 28

Du Pont arrested for murder of Olympic wrestler

John Eleuthere du Pont, a member of one of the richest families in the US, was arrested today, suspected of killing the Olympic gold-medal wrestler Dave Schultz.

Schultz was shot dead on Friday at John du Pont's estate at Newton Square, Pennsylvania. The arrest came after a 48-hour standoff between du Pont and police. Du Pont, an expert marksman, had barricaded himself inside his mansion. He was grabbed when he came outside to inspect his boiler, which the police had switched off.

Du Pont built the Delaware Museum of Natural History and managed the US Olympic pentathlon team in 1976. The millionaire is also a wrestling enthusiast, and he used his fortune to build and fund an Olympic training centre for wrestlers on his estate. Schultz was one of a team of athletes living and training there.

But du Pont is also known for his eccentric behaviour, which neighbours claimed had worsened in recent months. Allegations are emerging that last year du Pont banned African-American athletes from his estate, claiming that the colour black reminded him of death. (→ May 31)

JERUSALEM, SUNDAY 28

Ethiopian Jews riot over Israeli AIDS policy

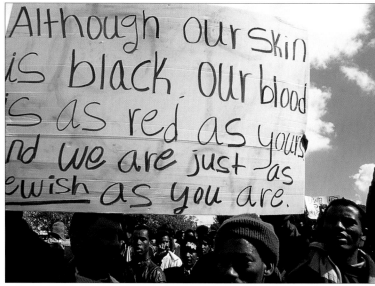

Ethiopian Jews protesting at what they perceive as racism in Israel's AIDS policy.

In Jerusalem today riot police fought with Ethiopian Jews who were angered by the revelation that Ethiopian blood was being dumped from Israeli blood banks.

Tear-gas and water cannon were used in an effort to disperse the crowd, which had surrounded the office of Prime Minister Shimon Peres. Protestors retaliated by throwing rocks, smashing car windows, and injuring dozens of police. The fighting lasted for several hours.

The authorities claim that blood donated by Ethiopians has too high a risk of infection from the HIV virus that causes AIDS. The Ethiopians, 60,000 of whom have arrived in Israel since 1984, believe they are victims of primitive racism. They claim they are also discriminated against in housing and employment.

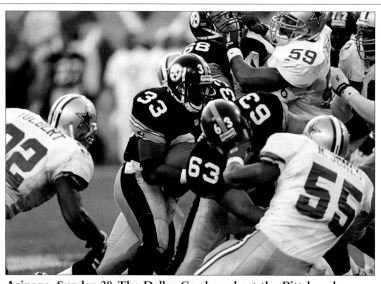

Arizona, Sunday 28. The Dallas Cowboys beat the Pittsburgh Steelers 27-17 in Super Bowl XXX, watched by TV viewers in 150 countries. It was the Cowboys' third Super Bowl win in four years.

LONDON, MONDAY 29

Camden council workers scoop the lottery

A syndicate of 33 council workers in the north London borough of Camden has won £10 million on the National Lottery. Working at Camden's homeless person's unit, the lottery winners spend their days helping some of society's neediest individuals find accommodation.

Although each winner is more than £300,000 better off today, the staff of the homeless unit turned up for work as usual. Margie West, an assessment officer, told reporters: "You can't just walk away from people who need you."

COLOMBO, SRI LANKA, WEDNESDAY 31

Tamil Tigers devastate capital

Colombo's Central Bank – the bomb blasted a 2.5-m (8-ft) crater in front of the building.

The wounded are carried to safety; more than 1,400 people were injured.

The Liberation Tigers of Tamil Eelam carried out a devastating terrorist attack on the Sri Lankan capital, Colombo, today. A truck loaded with 180 kg (400 lb) of explosives was driven through the gates of the Central Bank, in the heart of the city, at 10:45 a.m. The explosion caused widespread destruction, killing at least 55 people immediately. The death toll is expected to rise.

The majority of Sri Lankans are Sinhalese, the minority Tamil. For 13 years the Tamil Tigers have been fighting for a separate Tamil state. Recently the Sri Lankan army has scored successes against the Tigers. This was their response. (→ July 24)

WASHINGTON, DC, MON. 29

Russian says reforms go on

Russian prime minister Viktor S. Chernomyrdin, in Washington for a regular committee meeting with US vice president Al Gore, is insisting that economic and political reforms in Russia will continue.

Doubts have been cast over the reform programme's fate since leading economic reformer, Deputy Prime Minister Anatoli Chubais, resigned earlier this month. Russia needs a $9-billion IMF loan that will be blocked if doubts about reform persist.

Prime Minister Viktor S. Chernomyrdin

BELFAST, TUESDAY 30

Terrorist gunned down in West Belfast

Gino Gallagher, alleged to be the head of the Marxist Republican group, the Irish National Liberation Army (INLA), was shot dead by a gunman in a social security office on the Falls Road, West Belfast, today.

The INLA sees itself as a more radical alternative to the IRA's brand of Irish nationalism, and has been responsible for many terrorist acts in recent years.

No one has admitted responsibility for Gallagher's murder. Armed protestant groups have reportedly tried to kill him in the past, but the police believe he is more likely to have been the victim of a feud within the INLA itself. The murder does not directly threaten the continuation of the peace process in Northern Ireland, but it has led to renewed calls for the disarming of all political groups in the province.

BOSNIA, MONDAY 29

Three British soldiers killed by land-mine

Yesterday Britain suffered its first fatalities in Bosnia this year when an armoured personnel carrier drove into an unmarked minefield and was destroyed. The vehicle's three-man crew are presumed dead, but their bodies have not yet been retrieved because of heavy snow. A second vehicle involved in reconnaissance was able to pull back after the blast.

About 13,000 British troops are in Bosnia as part of the NATO force, known as I-FOR, which is attempting to ensure implementation of the Dayton peace accord.

Venice, Tuesday 30. The 204-year-old Fenice opera house, said to be the most beautiful in the world, was gutted by fire. "The whole world of opera feels like an orphan," Pavarotti told reporters. (→ June 26)

February

S	M	T	W	T	F	S
				1	2	3
4	5	6	7	8	9	10
11	12	13	14	15	16	17
18	19	20	21	22	23	24
25	26	27	28	29		

Yorkshire, 1
In the Hemsworth by-election, Arthur Scargill's Socialist Labour party wins only 5 per cent of the vote. The Labour party candidate, Jon Trickett, wins with 72 per cent.

London, 1
Leyton Orient defender Roger Stanislaus is suspended from football for a year for taking cocaine on the day of a match.

Yeovil, 2
A firebomb attack incinerates Liberal Democrat leader Paddy Ashdown's car outside his home in Somerset.

Bristol, 4
Firefighter Fleur Lombard is killed in a blaze in Bristol. She is the first woman firefighter to die on duty in Britain.

Dublin, 5
Mick McCarthy, former manager of Millwall, takes over as manager of the Republic of Ireland football team.

London, 6
British Gas announces the proposed early retirement of controversial chief executive Cedric Brown with a retirement package allegedly worth more than £4 million.

Heathrow, 6
Sarah Cook, the 13-year-old who married a Turkish waiter, returns to Britain from Turkey. (→ October 1)

Dominican Republic, 7
A Boeing 757 airliner crashes in the Caribbean, killing 189 people, mostly German tourists.

Westminster, 7
Labour leader Tony Blair announces that, if elected, his party will abolish the voting rights of hereditary peers in a reform of the House of Lords.

City of London, 8
Express newspapers, headed by Lord Stevens, and MAI, led by Lord Hollick, announce a £3 billion merger.

Luton, 9
Lord Brocket, a friend of the Prince of Wales, is jailed for five years for a £4.5 million insurance fraud.

Deaths
February 8. Derek Worlock, Roman Catholic Archbishop of Liverpool, in Liverpool, aged 76.

Docklands blast shatters the ceasefire

The bomb blows out windows of buildings on the Isle of Dogs and shakes the 250-m (800-ft) tall Canary Wharf tower.

Just after 7 p.m. today, the IRA ceasefire that had brought peace to the British Isles for 17 months came to a sudden and violent end. A bomb planted by the IRA exploded near South Quays railway station on the Isle of Dogs, devastating a swathe of London's Docklands.

The massive blast was heard up to 13 km (8 miles) away. Although warnings had been given, hundreds of people were still in the area when the bomb went off. Two have died and many more are injured.

The IRA declared it had ended the ceasefire "with great reluctance", claiming it had been driven to it by British "bad faith". Sinn Fein president Gerry Adams said he regretted the breakdown of the ceasefire, but he refused to condemn the bombing.

British prime minister John Major vowed to continue the search for peace. He said: "It would be a tragedy if the hopes of the people of Britain and Northern Ireland for a lasting peace were dashed again by the men of violence." (→ February 12)

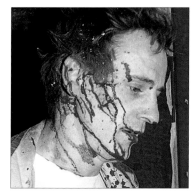

Most victims are injured by flying glass.

Beverly Hills, California, Friday 2. Gene Kelly, star of the musical, *Singin' in the Rain*, dies, aged 83.

Start of private passenger train service marred by ticket fraud

LTS Rail, the private company chosen to run train services on the London, Tilbury, and Southend line, had its franchise withdrawn this evening. The company is accused of a ticket fraud that cost London Transport £45,000 in lost revenue.

Two other private companies did start running passenger rail services this week – South Western Trains and Great Western Trains. They were operating the first private passenger trains in Britain for half a century. The allotment of a franchise to South Western Trains has also been criticized. The company is owned by Stagecoach, which operates coaches on routes in direct competition with the rail services it will be running.

Transport Secretary Sir George Young said he hoped people would look back on the start of private passenger services as "the point at which the renaissance of the railways began".

SARAJEVO, BOSNIA, TUESDAY 6

Serb officers suspected of war crimes are arrested

Arrested officers Colonel Aleksa Krsmanovic (left) and General Djordje Djukic.

Two senior Bosnian-Serb officers, General Djukic and Colonel Krsmanovic, have been detained in Sarajevo. The Bosnian government claims they were responsible for the massacre of civilians during the Bosnian war. The officers may stand trial before the War Crimes Tribunal in The Hague.

The Bosnian-Serb authorities have responded to the move by threatening not to implement the Dayton peace accord. (→ February 13)

WESTMINSTER, TUESDAY 6

Lords vote for free TV sport

The House of Lords tonight voted to save key sporting events from pay television. In an amendment to the government's Broadcasting Bill, peers insisted that the "crown jewels" of sport must be available free of charge to all television viewers.

The eight listed events are the Derby and the Grand National, the FA Cup and Scottish Cup finals, the football World Cup, the Wimbledon tennis tournament, home cricket test matches, and the Olympic Games.

The vote was a setback for Rupert Murdoch's BSkyB satellite television and for the government, which had wanted rights to all sports events open to commercial bidding. Labour spokesman Lord Donoughue called the vote "a tremendous victory for the British sporting public". The government is unlikely to try to overturn the amendment.

Philadelphia, Saturday 10. Chess champion Garry Kasparov lost the first game of his six-game tournament against computer Deep Blue. (→ February 17)

LOUISIANA, WEDNESDAY 7

Buchanan victory upsets Gramm

Pat Buchanan emerged as the leading conservative contender for the Republican presidential nomination by winning the Louisiana caucuses at the expense of Phil Gramm. Both belong to the anti-abortion, isolationist wing of the Republican party. Gramm was relying on support in the South to boost his campaign and had expected to do well in Louisiana.

Neither senator Bob Dole nor the other leading contender for the Republican candidacy, millionaire Steve Forbes, contested the Louisiana caucuses. (→ February 14)

BRITAIN, TUESDAY 6

Global freezing hits Britain

Much of Britain has been swept by blizzards for the last two days. The snow has brought chaos and power failures to the Scottish Borders, Cumbria, Wales, and the Midlands.

But Britons can take heart from a comparison with conditions elsewhere. In the US, at Ely, Minnesota, earlier this week, a temperature of -46°C (-51°F) was recorded.

Britain's freeze has been outdone by the United States. Chicago is deep in snow.

RUSSIA, SATURDAY 3

Yeltsin buys off striking miners

Yeltsin (right) touring Russian mines.

Russian president Boris Yeltsin has been forced to promise Russian miners back pay and subsidies worth around £3 billion to persuade them to end a national strike.

Some 450,000 miners – 80 per cent of the industry's workforce – had come out in support of their union's demands. The strike lasted two days.

These concessions are another blow to Yeltsin's prestige, and underline doubts as to whether he can carry through the tough financial cutbacks being demanded by the IMF.

Guatemala, Monday 5. Pope John Paul II was welcomed by thousands of Catholics during his two-day tour of the country.

February

Scott report puts ministers on the rack

Heading the inquiry – Sir Richard Scott.

Treasury Secretary, William Waldegrave.

Attorney General, Sir Nicholas Lyell.

The publication of the long-awaited Scott-inquiry report sparked furious debate in the House of Commons today. The government, which had given itself eight days to study the 1,800-page report before making it public, insisted it vindicated ministers' behaviour. The opposition were sure the document revealed shameful dishonesty and deception.

Sir Richard Scott was appointed to head the inquiry after the collapse of the trial of directors of the Matrix Churchill company, who had been accused of supplying arms to Iraq despite a government embargo. The report confirms that guidelines on the sale of arms to Iraq had been relaxed without the knowledge of parliament or the public, and that information had been wrongfully withheld from the defence in the Matrix Churchill trial.

The report is especially critical of William Waldegrave, the Chief Secretary to the Treasury, and Sir Nicholas Lyell, the Attorney General. Prime Minister John Major has rejected calls for the ministers' resignations. (→ February 26)

Joan Collins wins $3 million from publisher

Joan Collins celebrates her partial victory.

Actress and popular novelist Joan Collins is an estimated $3 million richer today after winning a legal battle with publisher Random House. The publisher had claimed that two manuscripts submitted by Ms. Collins were so badly written they were unpublishable and could not be called "complete". The contract for the two books was worth $4 million.

The jury found that the first work, *The Ruling Passion*, was complete, although the second, *Hell Hath No Fury*, was not. Presiding Judge Ira Gammerman said the case had been "a joy". Ms. Collins went off to celebrate with champagne.

Dayton accord on brink of failure

US Assistant Secretary of State Richard C. Holbrooke, who last year brokered the Dayton accord that stopped the Bosnian war, was back in the former Yugoslavia this weekend, striving to keep the peace alive.

Bosnian Serbs were threatening to return to confrontation after the arrest of two officers, Colonel Aleksa Krsmanovic and General Djordje Djukic. The men were flown to The Hague today, where they will face the International War Crimes Tribunal.

Holbrooke papered over the crisis by laying down rules covering future arrests. Only those on a list of 52 wanted men may be apprehended. The list includes Bosnian-Serb leaders Radovan Karadzic and General Ratko Mladic. (→ February 17)

Minneapolis, Thursday 15. The singer formerly known as Prince has married Myte Garcia, a Puerto Rican dancer. Myte referred to the star during the ceremony by pointing to his symbol.

BELFAST, MONDAY 12

Thousands join Irish peace rally

Many of the 3,000-strong crowd wave paper cut-outs of the dove, symbol of peace.

Thousands gathered outside Belfast City Hall to express the desire of the people of Northern Ireland for peace. They were responding to the IRA bombing last week that ended an 18-month ceasefire.

The British prime minister, John Major, gave his own response to the renewed terrorist campaign in a sombre five-minute television broadcast. He said that Sinn Fein, the political wing of the IRA, would be excluded from negotiations on the future of Northern Ireland until the ceasefire was reinstated. "The IRA will never bomb their way to the negotiating table," he said. But he insisted that the search for peace would continue.

Major is keen to hold elections as a prelude to negotiations, although the Irish leader, John Bruton, said that this would only serve to "pour petrol on the flames". (→ February 15)

MOSCOW, SUNDAY 11

Zhirinovsky flirts with extremists

Ultra-nationalist Vladimir Zhirinovsky today launched his campaign for the Russian presidency with a lavishly staged silver-wedding ceremony at Moscow's Church of St. Michael the Archangel. The star guest was Jean-Marie Le Pen, French National Front leader. Zhirinovsky hopes to boost his prestige by an alliance with European right-wing extremists.

Vladimir Zhirinovsky with wife Galina.

RIO DE JANEIRO, SUNDAY 11

Michael Jackson video made in Rio slums arouses controversy

Michael Jackson delights residents of Santa Marta during filming of his new video.

Pop superstar Michael Jackson began filming his latest music video in the slums of Rio de Janeiro today. Directed by Spike Lee, the video "They Don't Care About Us" is set in Santa Marta, one of Rio's *favelas* – crowded shantytowns that tumble chaotically down the steep hillsides.

The poverty of Santa Marta is not the image of Rio that the Brazilian authorities want the world to see. Soccer hero Pele, now minister of sport, said the video could harm Rio's bid for the 2004 Olympics. But legal action to stop the filming failed.

The people of Santa Marta are pleased. A local residents' spokesman said: "Thanks to Michael Jackson, our slum is now on the map. His visit here makes a world of difference."

PHILADELPHIA, SATURDAY 17

Kasparov wins "for the human race"

World chess champion Garry Kasparov triumphed over Deep Blue, the top chess computer, at the Pennsylvania Convention Center today. He won the sixth and final game of the eight-day challenge match to finish overall winner by four points to two.

Deep Blue, which can analyse 100 million chess positions a second, had shocked the chess world by defeating Kasparov in the match's first game. The human player then showed superior adaptability, changing his play to exploit the computer's weaknesses.

Afterwards, Kasparov said: "I did a good job for chess first, and probably for mankind." Kasparov had earlier declared that he was playing to defend "human dignity" against the machine.

CALCUTTA, SUNDAY 11

Cricket World Cup defies politics

The sixth cricket World Cup was inaugurated with a colourful ceremony in front of 110,000 people in Eden Gardens, Calcutta, tonight.

The opening of the competition has been overshadowed by the West Indies and Australia's refusal to play matches in Sri Lanka. They claim the security situation is too poor after a terrorist bomb wrecked the capital's centre two weeks ago. Australia and the West Indies will forfeit the two matches, giving Sri Lanka a four-point start in the qualifying round. (→ February 29)

Liverpool, Wednesday 14. Bob Paisley, manager of Liverpool football club from 1977 to 1983, died today, aged 77.

February

S	M	T	W	T	F	S
				1	2	3
4	5	6	7	8	9	10
11	12	13	14	15	16	17
18	19	20	21	22	23	24
25	26	27	28	29		

London, 18
Dame Judi Dench becomes the first person to win two Olivier awards in the same year. She wins best actress for *Absolute Hell* and best actress in a musical for *A Little Night Music*.

Gabon, 18
The World Health Organization sends experts to a village in Gabon where ten people have died of the Ebola virus after eating a chimpanzee.

Redditch, Worcestershire, 21
Lorry driver Stuart Morgan is charged with the murder of student Celine Figard last December. He pleads not guilty. (→ October 16)

Strasbourg, 21
The European Court of Human Rights unanimously rules that Home Secretary Michael Howard was in breach of human rights when he ordered the juvenile killers of James Bulger to be detained indefinitely. (→ July 30)

Riyadh, 21
King Fahd of Saudi Arabia announces that he is resuming full royal duties.

Los Angeles, 21
US Rap singer Snoop Doggy Dog, real name Calvin Broadus, and his bodyguard are cleared of the murder of Philip Woldemariam.

Arles, France, 21
Jeanne Calment, 121 years old today, and believed to be the oldest person ever, has released a pop CD to celebrate her birthday.

Paris, 22
President Jacques Chirac announces that France is to end conscription and scrap its land-based nuclear weapons.

London, 22
Peter Clowes, who defrauded 18,000 investors of £16 million, is freed on parole after serving four years of a ten-year prison term.

New Delhi, 22
Indian police charge 14 senior politicians with corruption, including four former ministers. Three other former ministers are already facing charges.

Deaths
February 20. Lord Marshall of Goring, British nuclear scientist and administrator, aged 63.

IRAQ, FRIDAY 23
Returning Iraqi defectors killed

Two sons-in-law of Iraqi president Saddam Hussein were killed today, only three days after returning to Iraq from exile in Jordan. Lieutenant-General Hussein Kamel and his brother Saddam Kamel had defected six months ago, vowing to overthrow Saddam Hussein.

The defectors returned to Iraq with their wives after Saddam promised they would be unharmed. Madeleine Albright, US ambassador to the UN, blamed Saddam for the killings, saying "his brutality knows no bounds".

Lahore, Thursday 22. As a guest of Imran and Jemima Khan, the Princess of Wales today visited the Shaukat Kanum cancer hospital, and later attended a party marking the end of the Muslim fast of Ramadan. (→ April 14)

LONDON, SUNDAY 18
Bus blown up by IRA in central London

The wreckage of the 171 double-decker bus that was torn apart last night by an IRA bomb.

A powerful explosion ripped apart a double-decker bus in central London last night, killing at least one person. The dead man is believed to be the bomber, whose explosive device went off prematurely.

The explosion occurred at 10:38 p.m. Fortunately the bus was almost empty and there were few passers-by. Coming only nine days after the Docklands bombing, it confirms that the IRA ceasefire is dead and buried.

MILFORD HAVEN, WEDNESDAY 21
Crippled tanker pollutes the Welsh coast

Around 150 people are involved in the clean-up operation on Pembrokeshire beaches.

An oil slick almost 65 km (40 miles) long was drifting along the west coast of Britain tonight as salvage experts at last brought the stricken tanker *Sea Empress* to safety.

The *Sea Empress* had run on to rocks six days ago while trying to enter the Pembrokeshire port of Milford Haven. Gales and high seas repeatedly frustrated salvage efforts and about half the tanker's 140,000-tonne cargo spewed into the sea.

The oil has already polluted a long stretch of the Pembrokeshire coast, blackening beaches and threatening wildlife, including seal colonies and tens of thousands of seabirds.

Tory majority reduced to two

Conservative MP Peter Turnham tonight announced he was resigning the party whip. He said he had been disturbed by the prime minister's handling of the Scott report and the failure to ask the ministers most criticized in the report to resign.

Mr. Turnham is the third Tory MP to quit in six months. His defection reduces the Tory majority to two.

Former Tory MP Peter Turnham.

Black workers were replaced by whites in Ford photograph

The Ford motor company has paid £1,500 compensation to each of four black assembly workers at its Dagenham plant after they were transformed into whites in a company promotional photograph.

The original group photograph of black and white Ford workers, taken in 1991, was used in publicity stressing the ethnic mix of Ford's workforce. Later, an advertising company employed by Ford to put together a campaign targetted at the Polish market used computer technology to put white faces on top of the black ones, presenting an image of an all-white Ford workforce.

The workers noticed the alterations when the doctored photograph was mistakenly used on the cover of a sales brochure created for the UK.

Pat Buchanan wins sensational victory in New Hampshire

Right-wing Republican candidate Pat Buchanan on the campaign trail.

Senate leader Bob Dole was licking his wounds after losing the New Hampshire primary yesterday. The right-wing commentator Patrick J. Buchanan topped the poll, beating Dole by a single percentage point, and throwing the contest for the Republican nomination wide open.

Buchanan's success has goaded Dole into a vituperative response. "This is now a race between the mainstream and the extreme," Dole said today, claiming that Buchanan's campaign displayed an "intolerance which I will not tolerate".

Buchanan rejects Dole's charge of extremism. "We are conservatives of the heart," he asserted. "We care about the people." (→ February 27)

Scientists discover the cause of addiction to cigarette smoking

The science journal *Nature* reports that a team of scientists led by Dr. Joanna Fowler at Brookhaven National Laboratory in New York state believe they have identified the mechanism of cigarette addiction.

According to the report, smoking reduces by an average 40 per cent the quantity of an enzyme, monoamine oxidase B, found in the brain. This increases the quantity of dopamine, a signalling chemical that helps regulate mood, movement, and the reinforcement of behaviour patterns. High levels of dopamine are associated with almost all addictive drugs.

Potgietersrus, South Africa, Thursday 22. Armed police protect black pupils entering the formerly whites-only Potgietersrus primary school as South Africa integrates its education system.

Brit music awards disrupted by Cocker protest

The Brit Awards were marked tonight by an incident involving Michael Jackson and Jarvis Cocker, lead singer of the British group, Pulp.

Jackson was performing his hit "Earth Song", accompanied by a group of children, when Cocker leaped on the stage and tried to disrupt the show. Cocker was arrested but released on bail. He vehemently denies an allegation that he attacked three of the children on stage.

Cocker later said: "My actions were a form of protest at the way Michael Jackson sees himself as some Christ-like figure with the power of healing. The music industry allows him to indulge his fantasies...I find it insulting to be accused of assaulting children. All I was trying to do was make a point." The awards ceremony will be broadcast on TV tomorrow evening without Cocker's interruption.

Oasis won the awards for best British group, best British album, and best video. Michael Jackson was presented with a specially created award for artist of a generation. There were no prizes for Pulp.

February

S	M	T	W	T	F	S
				1	2	3
4	5	6	7	8	9	10
11	12	13	14	15	16	17
18	19	20	21	22	23	24
25	26	27	28	29		

Washington, DC, 25
According to US intelligence sources, Libyan leader Colonel Gaddafi is building an underground chemical weapons plant inside a mountain.

Sierra Nevada, Spain, 25
In the World Alpine Ski Championships, Italian skier Alberto Tomba wins the men's slalom. He has already won the giant slalom.

Berlin, 26
The best film award at the Berlin Film Festival is won by Taiwanese director Ang Lee's version of Jane Austen's *Sense and Sensibility*. It stars Emma Thompson, who wrote the screenplay.

London, 26
An armed guard is put on Buckingham Palace as it is revealed that the royal family is a target for the renewed IRA terrorist campaign.

London, 26
Harrod's owner Mohamed Al Fayed and his brother lose their fight for British citizenship. Their application has been rejected by Home Secretary Michael Howard. (→ November 13)

London, 27
The Labour party calls for a revamp of comprehensive education to give a better deal to exceptional pupils.

London, 28
Prime Minister John Major and Irish premier John Bruton agree a timetable for the continuing Irish peace process. All-party talks on the future of Northern Ireland are set for June 10. (→ March 4)

Lumberton, North Carolina, 29
Daniel Green is found guilty of the murder of James R. Jordan, father of US basketball star Michael Jordan.

Bangkok, 28
English teacher Sandra Gregory is given a 25-year prison sentence in Thailand for drug-smuggling.

Pune, India, 29
In the cricket World Cup, the West Indies are defeated by Kenya, one of the greatest upsets in the history of the competition. (→ March 9)

Deaths
February 27. Pat Smythe, British showjumper, aged 67.

CAPE CANAVERAL, MONDAY 26

Satellite breaks free from space shuttle

A $442-million satellite was lost in space today when the 20-km- (12-mile-) long tether linking it to the space shuttle Columbia snapped. The tethered satellite was designed to generate electricity as the shuttle pulled it across the Earth's magnetic field. Researchers who had spent ten years developing the system were devastated by the setback.

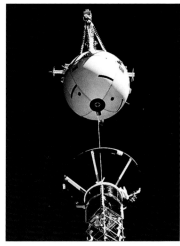

The tethered satellite.

LONDON, WEDNESDAY 28

Princess Diana agrees to give Charles a divorce

The front page of every daily paper declares the long-awaited news of the royal divorce.

At a meeting in St. James's Palace today, the Princess of Wales agreed to Prince Charles's request for a divorce. The royal couple had been strongly urged to divorce by the Queen last December. At present, Princess Diana would still become Queen if Charles succeeded to the throne.

A statement issued by the Princess said: "The Princess will continue to be involved in all decisions relating to the children and will remain at Kensington Palace." She will be known as "Diana, Princess of Wales". The Queen said she was "most interested" by the announcement. (→ July 5)

LOS ANGELES, THURSDAY 29

Seal and Alanis scoop Grammys

The usually staid Grammy awards sprang surprises this evening. Black British singer Seal won three awards, including song of the year for "Kiss from a Rose". The other big winner was the Canadian singer-songwriter Alanis Morisette, whose four awards included album of the year for her provocative *Jagged Little Pill*.

Seal at the Grammy awards ceremony.

Los Angeles, Sunday 25. Cambodian actor Haing Ngor (above right) has been shot dead outside his home in the Chinatown area of Los Angeles. A refugee who survived captivity and torture under the Khmer Rouge, Ngor won an Oscar for his role in the movie *The Killing Fields*. Police have as yet no idea why he was killed.

UN denounces Cuba for downing two planes flown by Cuban exiles

The UN Security Council today issued a statement "strongly deploring" Cuba's shooting down of two unarmed planes. The condemnation falls far short of what Cuban-Americans feel is required. Tough new economic sanctions against Cuba announced by President Clinton yesterday have also failed to Cuban satisfy the exile community.

The unarmed Cessna 337s were shot down on Saturday by Cuban MiG fighters, just outside Cuban territorial waters. All four people on board are presumed dead. The aircraft were flown by pilots belonging to Brothers to the Rescue, a Cuban exile group founded by Jose Basulto. They were apparently looking for small boats and rafts attempting to cross the strait from Cuba to Florida.

President Clinton has described the downing of the two aircraft as "a flagrant violation of international law". New measures against Cuba will include tightening the US's economic blockade and a block on tourist charter flights to the country from the US.

The anger of Cuban exiles at the downing of the aircraft has been partially diverted on to a traitor from their own ranks. Juan Pablo Roque, formerly a prominent member of Brothers to the Rescue, appeared on Cuban television to denounce the exile organization as a CIA-backed group that has repeatedly overflown Cuba expressly to note targets for sabotage. (→ March 12)

President Fidel Castro faces up to new economic sanctions against his country.

Tombstone, Arizona, Tuesday 27. On the campaign trail for the Arizona primary, Republican presidential candidate Pat Buchanan poses as a gunslinger at the famous OK Corral. But the Buchanan bandwagon is faltering. In the primaries today, he only came third in Arizona and North Dakota, and second in South Dakota. (→ March 5)

Tories win vote on Scott report by majority of one

John Major's government was saved from a humiliating defeat tonight by a last-minute change of heart on the part of a single Conservative MP, Rupert Allason. The MP had intended to join two of his colleagues, Quentin Davies and Richard Shepherd, in voting with the opposition at the end of the Commons debate on the Scott report. Had he done so, the government would have lost, with the chance of an early general election as a result.

The government had earlier refused to make concessions to David Trimble's Ulster Unionists on Northern Ireland, and the nine Unionist MPs also voted with the opposition.

Despite evident relief at their one-vote victory, the government emerged badly mauled from the debate. John Major has as usual put a brave face on the situation, saying: "Parliament has discussed Sir Richard Scott's report. Now it is time to get down to the detailed work of taking forward Sir Richard's recommendations."

Double suicide bombing in Israel kills 26

Terrorists killed 26 people and injured more than 80 in two bomb attacks in Israeli cities today.

The worst incident occurred in Jerusalem, where a device carried by a suicide bomber exploded on board a commuter bus, killing 24 people and injuring more than 50. In the second attack, a terrorist drove a car bomb into a crowd of soldiers at a hitch-hiking post in Ashkelon.

Hamas, the Islamic Resistance Movement, said it carried out the attacks to avenge the death of one of its members, Yahya Ayyash, in January.

Israeli prime minister Shimon Peres was jeered when he visited the site of the bus bomb. Many Israelis view the peace process, to which Peres is committed, as exposing the country to terrorism. (→ March 4)

Miami, Thursday 29. English golfer Nick Faldo spoke out today about his "month of hell" under the lash of the British tabloids. Last year the story broke that Faldo was leaving his wife and three children for 20-year-old Brenna Cepalak (above). Faldo recounts that he was under siege from journalists, with cameras trained on his house day and night. Now Faldo seems relaxed and ready to concentrate on his golf once more, in time for the US Masters. (→ April 14)

S	M	T	W	T	F	S
					1	2
3	4	5	6	7	8	9
10	11	12	13	14	15	16
17	18	19	20	21	22	23
24	25	26	27	28	29	30
31						

San Jose, California, 1
Researchers report that they have succeeded in transmitting a trillion bits of information a second through an optical fibre, equivalent to 12 million simultaneous phone calls.

Westminster, 1
Labour shadow Welsh Secretary Ron Davies apologizes for saying Prince Charles is not fit to be king.

The Hague, 1
Serb general Djordje Djukic is indicted for war crimes by the Hague tribunal. (→ March 22)

Hong Kong, 3
John Major visits the British colony and announces visa-free entry to Britain for millions of Hong Kong citizens after the Chinese takeover.

Little Rock, Arkansas, 4
The Whitewater trial opens: on trial are Governor Jim Guy Tucker and two former business associates of President Clinton. (→ April 28)

Belfast, 4
Sinn Fein is barred from the first day of intensive talks on the future of the province. (→ May 31)

Geneva, 7
Swiss drug giants Sandoz and Ciba-Geigy merge to create Novaretis, the second biggest pharmaceuticals company in the world.

London, 8
A cut in interest base rates triggers a fall in mortgage rates to their lowest level in 30 years.

Twickenham, 9
Will Carling announces that he will step down as England rugby captain after the last international of the season. (→ March 16)

Deaths
March 3. Marguerite Duras, French novelist, in Paris, aged 81.

March 6. Simon Cadell, actor in BBC TV's Hi-de-Hi, aged 45.

March 6. Douglas Jay, Lord Jay of Battersea, Labour politician, aged 89.

March 9. George Burns, comedian, in Beverly Hills, aged 100.

Researchers succeed in cloning sheep

A perfect pair: Cloned sheep Megan and Morag at Edinburgh's Roslin Institute.

To most people, all sheep look alike. But Welsh mountain sheep Megan and Morag are more alike than others. They are clones – identical animals produced by human ingenuity.

According to the journal *Nature*, researchers working at the Roslin Institute in Edinburgh took genetic material from a sheep embryo cell and placed it in an unfertilized ewe's egg from which the maternal genes were removed. The fertilized cells were then put into the wombs of ewes that acted as surrogate mothers. The result has been five cloned sheep, of which Megan and Morag survive.

The researchers believe they can now create thousands of mammal clones, including humans if desired. They will be able to "manufacture" animals with desirable traits.

TEL AVIV, MONDAY 4

Israel stunned by festival bombing

Rescue workers on Dizengoff Street, the scene of Tel Aviv's shopping-mall bombing.

For the second time in two days, Palestinian suicide bombers have struck at the heart of Israel. On Sunday in Jerusalem a bus was blown up, killing 19 people. Today it was Tel Aviv's turn. A suicide bomber exploded a device outside a shopping mall crowded with families celebrating the festival of Purim. In a scene of unbearable carnage, 12 people were killed and 100 more injured. Some of the victims were children in fancy dress for the festival. The Islamic extremist organization Hamas has said it carried out both attacks.

Despite tough anti-terrorist measures, the Israeli government seems incapable of stemming a wave of bombings that has cost 56 lives in nine days. But under pressure from the Palestinian leader Yassir Arafat, Hamas today called for a halt to the campaign.

WESTMINSTER, SATURDAY 2

Ban on gays in the services stays

Servicemen apparently back the government in upholding a ban on gays in the armed forces. A Ministry of Defence review found that the majority of soldiers, sailors, and airmen objected to serving with homosexuals.

Explaining the need for a gay ban, Minister of Defence Michael Portillo said soldiers "are living virtually on top of each other" in confined spaces. The ban is certain to be contested in the European Court of Human Rights.

FAISALABAD, SATURDAY 9

England crash out of World Cup

England made an inglorious exit from the cricket World Cup today, losing by five wickets to Sri Lanka, a country only recently accepted into the full Test circuit. It was the first time England failed to reach the semifinals.

The future of England manager Ray Illingworth is in doubt after this disappointment, but he was sanguine about the result. "It's a sign that some other countries have caught up," he stated, "and that's not a bad thing for cricket." (→ March 17)

London, Friday 8. British woman Caroline Beale returns after 18 months in a US prison. She was arrested in New York trying to carry the body of her dead baby on to a flight to London. This week she admitted manslaughter to gain release for treatment in Britain.

SAN FRANCISCO, FRIDAY 8

Courts boost right-to-die campaign

Right-to-die campaigner Dr. Jack Kevorkian, acquitted in Michigan of assisted suicide.

In a landmark decision, a US Court of Appeals in San Francisco has ruled in support of doctor-assisted suicide. The court struck down a Washington state law making assisted suicide a federal crime, and argued that there exists a constitutional right to die with dignity at a time of one's choosing.

In another notable verdict, a Michigan jury today acquitted Dr. Jack Kevorkian of assisted suicide, although he admitted helping two terminally ill people to inhale carbon monoxide. Dr. Kevorkian argued that he intended to relieve suffering, not to cause death. It was the second time he had been acquitted under a Michigan law designed to stop his widely publicized actions. He declared the verdict "a tremendous stroke in favour of rationality".

CANBERRA, SUNDAY 3

Howard is new PM as Australia swings right

Australia ended 13 years of Labour government today as the Liberal-National coalition, led by John Howard, swept to victory in a general election. The coalition won a majority of more than 40 seats in the 148-seat House of Representatives.

The result means that Australia is unlikely to become a republic. Labour had wanted a president to replace the Queen as Australia's head of state.

Australian prime minister John Howard.

NEWBURY, FRIDAY 8

Newbury bypass protestors cleared from tree-tops

The battle of the Newbury bypass this week moved into the tree-tops, where protestors blocking the route of the new road have established a network of aerial walkways and tree houses.

Bailiffs are employing professional climbers to help clear the way for the bulldozers. Climbing with harnesses, they cut walkway ropes as tree surgeons sawed away at branches around the protestors. Potentially fatal struggles occurred 21 m (70 ft) off the ground as protestors and bailiffs' men wrestled and grappled.

One professional climber, Peter Bukowski, said he quit because he found the work too unpleasant and stressful. "I was getting covered in urine and ravioli which they were throwing at me," said Bukowski. The battle continues.

Kuala Lumpur, Saturday 9. The PETRONAS towers, under construction in Malaysia's capital, are already the tallest buildings in the world. Reaching 451.89 m (1,482.61 ft) above street level, the identical towers are 8.83 m (29 ft) taller than the previous record-holder, Chicago's Sears Tower.

23

March

Melbourne, 10
British driver Damon Hill wins the Australian Grand Prix, equalling his father Graham Hill's total of 14 Grand Prix victories. (→ April 7)

Johannesburg, 11
The trial opens of South African general Magnus Malan and 19 others accused of murder and conspiracy during the days of apartheid. (→ October 11)

Seoul, South Korea, 11
Two former presidents of South Korea, Chun Doo-hwan and Roh Tae-woo, go on trial charged with mutiny and treason for staging a coup in 1979 and ordering a massacre of protestors the following year. (→ August 26)

Brussels, 12
The European Court of Justice rules that Britain must accept an EC directive imposing a maximum 48-hour working week.

Geneva, 12
The World Health Organization sets up an obesity task force to combat an epidemic of obesity worldwide.

Washington, DC, 12
President Clinton signs the Helms-Burton bill tightening the US economic embargo on Cuba.

Washington, DC, 14
Steve Forbes officially withdraws from the race for the Republican presidential nomination. (→ March 19)

Cheltenham, 14
The Cheltenham Gold Cup is a triumph for Ireland as Imperial Call wins, trained by Fergie Sutherland and ridden by Conor O'Dwyer.

Jerusalem, 14
After attending an anti-terrorism summit in Egypt, President Clinton visits Israel and pledges $65 million to help Israel combat terrorist attacks.

Houston, Texas, 16
A study by researchers at the University of Houston suggests that around 300 Mexicans die attempting to cross into the US every year.

Deaths
March 13. Krzysztof Kieslowski, Polish film director, aged 54.

Bob Dole sweeps seven states as Perot gears up

Ross Perot, 1992 presidential candidate, addresses his Reform party supporters.

Senator Bob Dole is almost certain to be the Republican candidate in this year's US presidential election after victories in all seven primaries on Super Tuesday. His wins included Texas and Florida, which between them send 221 delegates to the Republican convention. Dole has now secured more than 700 delegates, compared with around 70 for remaining rivals Steve Forbes and Pat Buchanan. Two other contestants, Lamar Alexander and Richard Lugar, stepped down last week.

Steve Forbes is widely expected to announce his withdrawal from the race on Thursday. Despite spending millions in promotion, the maverick millionaire has won only two primaries, in Arizona and Delaware. Pat Buchanan has admitted that Dole's candidacy "appears inevitable", but is determined to continue the contest.

Meanwhile, Ross Perot's Reform party is working away in the wings to challenge both President Clinton and Dole. Perot won 19 per cent of the vote as an independent presidential candidate in 1992. This time he says he will not stand himself. But with the president dogged by scandal and Dole lacking charisma, a Reform party candidate might just make a mark. (→ March 14)

Carling farewell marred by injury

An ankle injury in the thirty-fifth minute brought Will Carling's last appearance as England rugby captain to an early end. But there was ample compensation in England's 28-15 victory over Ireland, which made them Five Nations champions for the fourth time under Carling's leadership. The French had been expected to take the trophy, but surprisingly they lost 16-15 to Wales at Cardiff.

Carling goes down with a twisted ankle.

Las Vegas, Saturday 16. Mike Tyson (right) becomes World Boxing Council heavyweight champion, defeating British titleholder Frank Bruno at the MGM Grand Garden arena. The fight was stopped 50 seconds into the third round of a one-sided contest. Bruno had held the title for 197 days.

DUNBLANE, WEDNESDAY 13

Massacre of the innocents at Dunblane

The massacred class of Dunblane Primary School: Teacher Gwenne Mayor (back row, left) and 16 children were killed; only one of the 29 children in the class escaped injury.

The worst multiple murder in modern British history brought horror and grief to the small Scottish town of Dunblane yesterday. A former Scout leader, Thomas Hamilton, shot dead 16 young children and a teacher in the local primary school before turning a gun upon himself.

The massacre happened just before 9:30 a.m. Hamilton walked into the school armed with four guns and forced his way into the gym, where a class of five- and six-year-olds were waiting to begin their exercises. The class's teacher, Gwenne Mayor, a part-time gym teacher, Eileen Harrild, and a supervisory assistant, Mary Blake, were in the room with the children.

Hamilton fired on the adults, killing Mrs. Mayor and wounding the two other adults. He then walked around the gym systematically shooting the children, killing 15 on the spot and fatally wounding one other. Only one child in the class escaped injury. After firing a volley into another classroom, fortunately hitting no one, Hamilton shot himself in the mouth.

Children's relatives rushed to Dunblane Primary School on hearing of the shooting.

Killer Thomas Hamilton.

Today the people of Dunblane are struggling to come to terms with the tragedy that has struck their quiet town. The headmaster of Dunblane Primary School, Ron Taylor, said: "Evil visited us yesterday and we don't know why. And we don't understand it and I guess we never will."

Thomas Hamilton was a local man, a loner with an interest in young boys and in guns. He seems to have been obsessed by his dismissal from the post of Scout leader in 1973. On the Friday before the killings, he wrote a letter to the Queen protesting against the damage the Scout Association had done to his reputation. In another letter of complaint, he specifically mentioned Dunblane Primary School. Although Hamilton was known to police because of complaints about his activities with boys' clubs, he had been issued with firearms certificates for all his weapons. (→ March 17)

DUNBLANE, MARCH 1996

Dunblane: anger and mourning

NO EVENT in recent times has wrung such an emotional response from the British people as the massacre of schoolchildren at Dunblane. On the Sunday after the killings, a minute's silence was observed across Britain. The Queen and the Princess Royal were visibly moved when they visited Dunblane that afternoon and spoke to relatives of the victims.

A whole nation's grief

Even politicians responded to the event with a rare dignity. In the House of Commons the day after the massacre, the shadow Scottish Secretary George Robertson, whose three children attended Dunblane Primary School, spoke most movingly of "the grief and the horror and the sheer desolation our town feels today". Party leaders John Major and Tony Blair set aside their differences to visit Dunblane side by side.

Mingled with the mourning, there was widespread anger at the ease with which Thomas Hamilton had been granted licences for an armoury of lethal weapons. MP Denis Canavan expressed the view of many people when he said: "This man was known for his erratic behaviour and instability. This should have been sufficient reason to refuse a firearms licence."

Searching for answers

Former Home Office minister David Mellor led calls for a complete ban on handguns. He called on people "to keep their anger burning bright" about the issue.

In the wake of the massacre, it was announced that an inquiry was to be set up, headed by Lord Cullen, a senior Scottish judge. The inquiry was bound to consider changes in fire-arms laws. But it seemed unlikely to unravel the mystery at the heart of the tragedy – how any human being could commit such an act of inhumanity.

Meanwhile, the people of Dunblane appealed for privacy to cope with their grief. The school's headmaster, Ron Taylor, expressed his community's will to live on. "Come back in a year", he told visiting political leaders, "and we will show you we have beaten this."

The town of Dunblane: "Come back in a year and we will show you we have beaten this."

A policeman is overcome during the minute's silence at 9:30 a.m. on Sunday 17 March.

Mourners outside Dunblane Cathedral.

The Queen and the Princess Royal lay a wreath outside Dunblane Primary School. They also met with the parents of the murdered children.

Dunblane Cathedral's overcrowded Sunday service was transmitted live to the nation.

Observing the one minute's silence.

The school's gym was later demolished.

"Evil visited us yesterday"

The killer, Thomas Hamilton, shot himself after the massacre.

Ron Taylor, the school's head: "I feel total devastation."

The children's teacher, Gwenne Mayor, also died in the massacre.

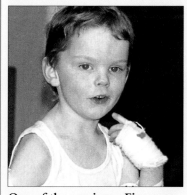

One of the survivors: Five-year-old Ben Vallance in hospital.

March

Dunblane, 17
The Queen visits the site of the Dunblane massacre. A minute's silence is observed throughout Britain. (→ May 29)

Rome, 17
The Italian *Serie A* football league programme is cancelled as players strike, demanding more say in how the game is run.

London, 19
Rosemary West loses her appeal against conviction for the murders in Cromwell Street, Gloucester.

Ohio, 19
Bob Dole sweeps the Mid-West primaries, effectively securing the Republican nomination. (→ May 15)

London, 20
Price-capping by the industry regulator Oftel on British Telecom charges is expected to cut £20 from average phone bills over five years.

Milan, 20
Opera singer Luciano Pavarotti owns up to an affair with his 26-year-old secretary and says he is leaving his wife after 35 years of marriage.

Los Angeles, 20
After a second trial, Lyle and Erik Menendez are found guilty of the shotgun murders of their parents in 1989. Their first trial in 1993-94 ended without a decision. (→ April 17)

Bangladesh, 20
Bangladeshi prime minister Khalida Zia agrees a bill for new elections to be held under a non-party government, as riots and strikes continue across the country.

The Hague, 22
The tribunal investigating war crimes in the former Yugoslavia makes its first indictment, of three Muslims and a Croat, for the murder, torture, and rape of Serb prisoners. (→ May 7)

London, 23
McDonald's announces it is banning British beef from its burgers. (→ March 25)

Deaths
March 17. Rene Clement, French film maker, aged 82.

STRASBOURG, FRIDAY 22

Europe bans British beef exports after minister's "mad cow" revelations

Health Secretary Stephen Dorrell: His speech raised the alarm over beef dangers.

Britain's beef industry was facing catastrophe this evening as experts talked of the possible slaughter of all 11 million British cattle, and 12 EU countries banned British beef as unsafe for human consumption.

The crisis broke on Wednesday when the Health Secretary, Stephen Dorrell, told Parliament of a possible link between bovine spongiform encephalopathy (BSE) in cattle – "mad cow" disease – and a new strain of Creutzfeldt-Jakob disease (CJD) in humans. Government advisers believe the possibility of a major CJD epidemic cannot be ruled out.

BSE was first discovered in British cattle in 1986. The disease is believed

John Niven, a Perthshire farmer, could lose his entire herd in the current BSE scare.

to have spread by feeding cows on offal from other animals. Measures were taken to extirpate the disease from cattle herds and prevent infection of humans, but critics claim the government response was too little, too late. Ministers appeared more concerned with reassuring consumers about the safety of eating beef – John

Gummer, then agriculture minister, even fed his daughter a beefburger in front of massed press cameras.

Today, many British consumers have reacted to the latest scare with a spontaneous boycott of beef on supermarket shelves. The European Commission will discuss the issue at a meeting on Monday. (→ March 23)

LONDON, SUNDAY 17

Bright blue rock from Morocco baffles the scientists

Anna Grayson shows off her discovery.

The Natural History Museum said today that a blue rock found on a stall in Morocco is a mineral previously unknown to science. The rock was bought by broadcaster Anna Grayson, who took it to the museum when presenting a programme there last year.

About 40 new minerals are identified every year, mostly in minute quantities. According to Dr. Gordon Cressey, this specimen is remarkable because of its size and colour. He described it as "the most strikingly blue mineral ever discovered".

LONDON, WEDNESDAY 20

Stonehenge is older than anyone thought

A conference at the Royal Society in London was told today that Stonehenge is probably 1,000 years older than was previously believed. Recent carbon dating of bone fragments found at the site show they are 5,000 years old. This means they date from before the building of the first pyramids in Egypt. The massive central stones that give the monument its awesome appearance are more recent, dating from around 2300BC.

TAIWAN, SATURDAY 23

Taiwan defies China and elects a president

Taiwan successfully held its first democratic presidential election today. The sitting president, Lee Teng-hui, scored a resounding victory, gathering 54 per cent of a vote that was split between four candidates.

But the true victory was that the vote happened at all. It marks the end of four decades of single-party rule on the island. And it marks a triumph over intimidation from mainland China, which staged military manoeuvres near Taiwan in the build-up to the election and threatened to invade the island if it declared independence.

In China's view, Taiwan is a rebellious province that must one day be reunited with mainland China. President Lee pays lip service to "one China", but in practice he governs Taiwan as an independent state.

The US had sent two aircraft carriers to Taiwan to counter Chinese threats and this week agreed to sell the Taiwanese a range of high-tech military equipment. (→ May 20)

Manila, Philippines, Tuesday 19. At least 150 people were killed in a fire at the Ozone disco, Quezon City. Most were teenagers celebrating the start of the school holidays. There was no fire exit and many were trampled to death in the rush to the only door.

Celebrating President Lee Teng-hui's victory in Taiwan's first democratic election.

SOUTH AFRICA, TUESDAY 19

Mandela speaks of his loneliness as divorce proceeds

Mandela: "I was the loneliest man."

South African president Nelson Mandela has been granted a divorce from his wife Winnie. The judge rejected Mrs. Mandela's argument that the president should submit to tribal mediation to save the marriage.

Yesterday, President Mandela told the court of the emptiness of his married life. "Ever since I returned from prison," he said, "not once has the defendant ever entered our bedroom whilst I was awake... I was the loneliest man during the period I spent with her." The president said he had been shown letters proving his wife's infidelity. Mrs. Mandela, whose expenses reportedly far exceed her income, is claiming half President Mandela's assets in settlement.

LAHORE, SUNDAY 17

Sri Lanka wins World Cup

A century from Aravinda de Silva saw Sri Lanka to a seven-wicket victory in the cricket World Cup final. Their opponents, Australia, who had refused to play in Sri Lanka at the start of the competition, were outclassed by a dazzling exhibition of spin bowling and classic strokeplay. Rejoicing fans filled the streets of the capital, Colombo, late into the night.

WESTMINSTER, WEDNESDAY 20

Howard proposes heavier sentences

New fixed minimum sentences for certain categories of criminal could increase the prison population by almost 20 per cent. Under proposals put forward by Home Secretary Michael Howard, burglars would receive a minimum three-year sentence for a third offence and drug dealers would face a minimum sentence of six years.

Paris, Tuesday 19. Michael Jackson and Saudi Prince al-Walid bin Talal, one of the world's richest investors, launch show-business venture Kingdom Entertainment, dedicated to "family values".

March

Wembley, 24
Aston Villa beats Leeds United 3-0 in the Coca-Cola Cup final.

Brussels and Westminster, 25
The European Commission imposes a worldwide ban on British beef exports. The UK government reacts angrily, refusing to order a mass slaughter of cattle and claiming that the risk of infection to humans is negligible. (→ March 28)

Washington, DC, 25
New $100 bills are delivered, the first major change in the design of the US currency since 1929.

Houston, 25
Comet Hyakutake, the brightest comet for 20 years, reaches its closest point to the Earth and is clearly visible to the naked eye.

San Francisco, 25
More than 100 gays are married in a mass ceremony sanctioned by the city authorities.

Luton, 26
Gaetano Costanza, a man who harassed a woman with letters and phone calls, is convicted of assault, although he never touched his victim.

Westminster, 28
The government announces the banning of meat and bonemeal in animal feed. (→ April 3)

Cyprus, 29
Three British soldiers found guilty of raping and killing a Danish woman, Louise Jensen, receive life sentences.

Paris, 29
Rugby League's European Super League plays its first match, in which Paris St. Germain beat the Sheffield Eagles 30-24.

Aintree, 30
The Grand National is won by Rough Quest, after a stewards' enquiry.

Deaths
March 26. John Snagge, BBC radio broadcaster, aged 91.

March 26. Former US senator Edmund S. Muskie, Democratic politician, in Washington, DC, aged 81.

Oscars for Scotland and a talking pig

Babe's visual effects team claims the only Oscar won by the hugely popular film.

Christopher Reeve's appearance onstage was greeted by tears and an ovation.

Five-time nominee Susan Sarandon wins best actress for her role in Dead Man Walking.

Tartan set the pattern for this year's Academy Awards, with a triumph for Mel Gibson's kilted epic *Braveheart*, a boisterous movie loosely based on the life of thirteenth-century Scottish patriot William Wallace. It won five Oscars, including best picture, and best director for Gibson.

Susan Sarandon won the best actress award for her role as a nun in *Dead Man Walking*. It was the fifth time she had been nominated, but only the first time she had won. The best actor award went to Nicolas Cage for his performance as an amoral suicidal alcoholic in *Leaving Las Vegas*, and Mira Sorvino won best supporting actress in *Mighty Aphrodite* as a dumb-blonde hooker.

Unfortunately not present at the award ceremony was Babe, the talking pig who wanted to be a sheep dog. One of the surprise movie successes of the last year, *Babe* won the award for best visual effects. Also absent was Oliver Stone, director of *Nixon*, who had ostentatiously chosen to spend the evening with Zapatista guerrillas in Mexico.

British successes included *A Close Shave*, starring Wallace and Gromit, which brought British animator Nick Park his third Oscar in five years for best short animated film. British actress Emma Thompson won an Oscar for best adaptation for her screenplay based on Jane Austen's *Sense and Sensibility*.

The most moving moments of the evening were courageous appearances by *Superman* star Christopher Reeve, paralysed in a riding accident last year, and Kirk Douglas, who recently suffered a stroke and struggled to deliver his speech accepting a special honorary award.

Braveheart sweeps the board, winning five Oscars, including one for best picture.

Israeli assassin is jailed for life

TEL AVIV, WEDNESDAY 27

Jewish extremist Yigal Amir was sentenced to life imprisonment today for the assassination of Israeli prime minister Yitzhak Rabin. He killed Rabin in an attempt to stop the Palestinian peace process. Amir told the court: "Everything I did was for the God of Israel, the Torah of Israel, the people of Israel and the land of Israel." Judge Edmond Levy said Amir had "lost all semblance of humanity".

Yitzhak Rabin's assassin, Yigal Amir— unrepentant in the face of a life sentence.

Houston, Monday 25. The Russian space station Mir and space shuttle Atlantis fly together through space after docking yesterday. Today American astronaut Shannon Lucid floated through the shuttle to the space station where she will live for the next five months. "I am happy to be here," she stated.

CAPE TOWN, MONDAY 25

IAAF ban on Modahl is lifted

British athlete Diane Modahl has won a 19-month fight to clear her name after failing a drug test. The International Amateur Athletic Federation (IAAF), meeting in Cape Town, has declared the test unreliable.

Modahl was banned from competition for four years in 1994 when a Lisbon laboratory testing a urine sample found evidence of steroid abuse. The British Athletic Federation set aside the ban last July after Modahl produced evidence that the sample had been left unrefrigerated. The IAAF decision completes her rehabilitation. A delighted Modahl said today: "It has been a costly fight...The powerful organizations in control of sport can make or break you. I believe there were those who wanted to break me."

GLEN CANYON, ARIZONA, MONDAY 25

Man-made flood to clean up US river

The flood's source: 117 billion gallons of water will be pumped through the canyon.

One of the boldest ecological experiments ever attempted began at dawn today. US interior secretary Bruce Babbitt pressed a button, pulled a lever, and turned a wheel to release a flood of water through the Glen Canyon dam into the Colorado river. Over the next week 117 billion gallons will surge through the Grand Canyon, imitating the regular spring floods that used to occur before the dam was built in 1963.

Scientists hope the artificial flood will cleanse and refresh the Colorado, reviving natural habitats and restoring the shoreline in the canyon. Some 200 observers are stationed along the river to monitor the varying effects of the flood. "This is about restoring one of the most amazing, most beautiful places on Earth," Babbitt said.

S	M	T	W	T	F	S
	1	2	3	4	5	6
7	8	9	10	11	12	13
14	15	16	17	18	19	20
21	22	23	24	25	26	27
28	29	30				

Westminster, 2
Emergency anti-terrorist measures are rushed through Parliament, giving police new powers to stop and search terrorist suspects.

London 2
The chief executive of the Woolwich Building Society, Peter Robinson, leaves the company after allegations of expense account discrepancies. He claims he has been the victim of a smear campaign.

Washington, DC, 3
General Norman Schwarzkopf, US commander in the Gulf War, and 14 other retired US officers call on the US government to institute a total ban on the use of landmines.

Westminster, 3
The government announces that a referendum will be held after the next general election to decide whether Britain should commit to a single European currency.

Washington, DC, 3
A two-year study by the US Defense Department finds no evidence of "Gulf War syndrome" afflicting soldiers who took part in the conflict. (→ October 1)

Seoul, South Korea, 5
South Korean and US troops go on alert after North Korea announces that it no longer recognizes the demilitarized zone that has separated it from the South since the Korean War.

London, 5
Authorities reveal that a test to determine whether people are HIV positive could be faulty. Some 60,000 people declared clear of infection may not be.

British Columbia, Canada, 5
Estranged husband Mark Vijay Chahal kills nine people at his former wife's wedding party, including his former wife, before killing himself.

Zimbabwe, 6
Zimbabwean vice-president, Joshua Nkomo, announces publicly that his son has died of AIDS. He says the disease is "harvested by whites to obliterate blacks".

Deaths
April 6. Greer Garson, movie actress, aged 92, in Dallas.

LONDON, WEDNESDAY 3

Birth-control jab for men unveiled

The World Health Organization today announced a breakthrough in birth control for men. An international team of scientists has developed and tested a weekly injection that reduces sperm production to a negligible level, while leaving sexual performance unimpaired.

Dr. Fred Wu of the University of Manchester, a member of the scientific research team, stated: "It is really for the first time showing the world that permanent contraception for men really works."

Moscow, Tuesday 2. Russian president Boris Yeltsin (right) and president of Belarus Alexander Lukashenko (left), today signed an accord linking their economies and political systems. The alliance was blessed by Russian Orthodox patriarch Alexei II.

LINCOLN, MONTANA, THURSDAY 4

Unabomber suspect arrested in Montana shack

In a one-room cabin 8 km (5 miles) outside the small town of Lincoln, Montana, the FBI yesterday apprehended a man they firmly believe to be the Unabomber, responsible for 16 bomb attacks in the last 17 years.

Theodore J. Kaczynski, a Harvard graduate and former mathematics assistant professor at Berkeley, now a dishevelled recluse, has been charged with possession of bomb-related materials. FBI agents are combing his tiny shack for evidence to link him to the Unabomber outrages.

The Unabomber's attacks have killed three people and injured 23. His main targets were universities, airlines, and computer stores. (→ April 13)

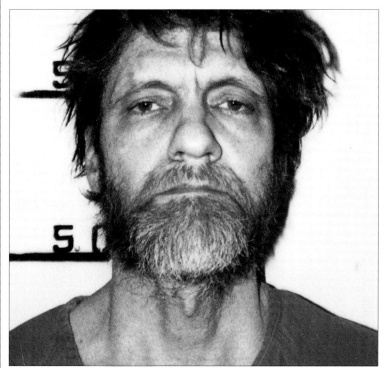

Suspect Theodore J. Kaczynski, arrested for possession of bomb-related materials.

SEAFORD, SUSSEX, FRIDAY 5

Tragic end for Hendrix's last lover

German-born Monika Danneman, aged 50, pledged her life to Hendrix's memory.

Monika Danneman, last girlfriend of rock guitarist Jimi Hendrix, was found dead in her fume-filled car today. Police said it was probably suicide.

Her death came 48 hours after the High Court found her guilty of contempt for repeating allegations that another former lover of Hendrix, Kathy Etchingham, was an "inveterate liar". The two women had long been in dispute, especially over the circumstances of Hendrix's death 26 years ago in Ms. Danneman's London flat.

Ms. Danneman led a reclusive life, turning her Sussex cottage into a shrine to the rock star. Ms. Etchingham said: "I am greatly saddened that it should have to end like this."

WESTMINSTER, WEDNESDAY 3

Britain caught in beef nightmare as European ban continues

Britain faces the prospect of slaughtering cattle on a massive scale in a desperate attempt to resolve the country's beef crisis.

It is two weeks since the British government revealed a possible link between "mad cow" disease found in some British cattle herds and a new strain of Creutzfeld-Jakob disease in humans. At first, the government rejected calls for a cull of millions of cattle, but the crisis will not go away.

Today, Britain failed to persuade the European Union to lift its worldwide ban on the export of British beef, despite offering to kill and burn all cattle over 30 months old. Europe is demanding more stringent measures, and even then will not promise to lift the ban until confidence is restored.

The British government is furious at European intransigence. Douglas Hogg, agriculture minister, said of the ban: "It is not justified. It is not based on scientific analysis." The European Union has, however, offered to help Britain compensate cattle farmers. (→ April 14)

Red Sea, Friday 5. The Cunard luxury liner Royal Viking Sun has limped into the Egyptian port Sharm el Sheikh after striking a coral reef in the Tiran Strait. One hundred and twenty of the passengers had been transferred from another Cunard ship that ran aground earlier in the year off the Philippines.

DELAWARE, SATURDAY 6

Clinton grieves for plane-crash victims

President Bill Clinton was at Dover Air Force Base, Delaware, today to mourn a friend who was also one of his closest political allies.

US Commerce Secretary Ron Brown was among 33 people killed when their plane crashed into a mountainside near Dubrovnik, Croatia, three days ago. The bodies were brought home in caskets draped with the Stars and Stripes.

Brown was the first African American to be elected chairman of the Democratic National Committee and the first appointed to head the Commerce Department. He was on a visit to Croatia and Bosnia to look for ways to back the rebuilding of the war-torn region. (→ April 12)

President Clinton comforts Alma Brown, widow of Commerce Secretary Ron Brown.

LONDON, FRIDAY 5

Oasis stars are nice, decent boys, says their mother

Liam and Noel Gallagher, stars of British rock band Oasis, have carefully cultivated a bad boy image. Last month Noel told the music paper *Melody Maker* that he and his brother "have burgled houses and nicked car stereos". There was an outcry from Tory MPs, and the police promised to investigate any crime that might have been committed.

But today Noel and Liam's mother, Margaret, painted a very different picture of the wild men of rock. Interviewed on BBC's *World at One*, she said: "As far as I know they were never involved in any crime at all.... Really they are very thoughtful and kind and all they think about are their family and friends."

LEEDS, SATURDAY 6

Serb war veteran dies after vicious street attack

Stevan Popovic, a Second World War veteran and a prominent member of the British Serb community, has died in hospital after being mugged in the Chapeltown district of Leeds.

Mr. Popovic, aged 74, had stopped to ask directions after he took a wrong turning. He was pulled from his car, kicked, and beaten. His attacker stole £50 in cash, a coat, a watch, and a wedding ring.

Gatwick, Tuesday 2. An Air France Concorde has been turned into an advertisement as part of Pepsi's "Project Blue", a $500-million campaign to revamp Pepsi's image. A new blue can is intended to mark Pepsi out as sharply different from its red rival, Coca-Cola.

Noel and Liam Gallagher claim to have been involved in crimes in the past.

April

S	M	T	W	T	F	S
	1	2	3	4	5	6
7	8	9	10	11	12	13
14	15	16	17	18	19	20
21	22	23	24	25	26	27
28	29	30				

Northern Ireland, 8
Riot police in Belfast open fire with plastic bullets after drunken loyalists attack RUC officers.

Rusk, Texas, 8
Child molester Larry Don McQuay is released from jail under strict parole terms. McQuay famously requested castration, threatening otherwise to rape and kill children on his release.

Dusseldorf, 9
At least 16 people are killed and 150 injured after a fire breaks out in one of the terminals at Dusseldorf airport.

Kuala Lumpur, 9
Nurse Pauline Robinson saves the life of British tennis hopeful Lucy Needham, who fell ill on a flight from Kuala Lumpur to Heathrow.

South Lebanon, 10
A Hizbollah mortar attack kills an Israeli soldier in south Lebanon. (→ April 13)

Cambridgeshire, 10
Ben Gunn, the chief constable of Cambridgeshire, is stopped for speeding at 145 kmph (90 mph) on the M11 by one of his own men.

Westminster, 11
In the Staffordshire South East by-election, the Tories are humiliated by a 22 per cent swing to Labour. The government's majority is reduced to one. (→ May 3)

Washington, DC, 11
President Clinton vetoes a bill that would ban late abortions.

Seoul, South Korea, 11
South Korean elections take away the government's majority in parliament. President Kim Young Sam's position is unthreatened, however.

Washington, DC, 12
Trade representative Mickey Kantor is named by Bill Clinton as commerce secretary to replace Ron Brown.

Lincoln, Montana, 13
Investigators claim to have discovered the original Unabomber manifesto in Theodore J. Kaczynski's cabin.

Deaths
April 9. Richard Condon, thriller writer, aged 81, in Dallas, Texas.

LONDON, THURSDAY 11
Another royal marriage splits

Marina Mowatt with her two children.

After the separation of Princess Anne and Captain Mark Phillips, the Prince and Princess of Wales, and the Duke and Duchess of York, the troubled marital affairs of the royal family took another twist today. Marina Mowatt, daughter of the Queen's cousin Princess Alexandra and Sir Angus Ogilvy, today announced her separation from her husband, Paul.

Marina Mowatt, who is thirtieth in line of succession to the throne, married her photographer husband in 1990, when she was six months pregnant. They have two children, aged six and three.

MONROVIA, THURSDAY 11
Westerners flee anarchy in strife-torn Liberia

US helicopters have begun ferrying Americans and other foreign nationals to safety as the West African state of Liberia descends into chaos.

Armed supporters of Liberian warlord Roosevelt Johnson went on the rampage in Monrovia after he was dismissed from the government and the Council of State ordered his arrest for murder. Members of the West African peacekeeping force, installed in Liberia at the end of a previous civil conflict, have reportedly joined in the looting.

Hundreds of foreign nationals have taken refuge in the US embassy compound, but many others are cut off in other parts of the country. A US naval force in the Mediterranean is being diverted to Liberia. (→ May 14)

Fighters in the Liberian conflict; Monrovia is described as a "frenzy of looting".

Los Angeles, Friday 12. Actor Marlon Brando (right) caused a stir last week when he told CNN's Larry King (left) that Hollywood had shown every racial stereotype except "the kike". Faced with a storm of protests over his comments, Brando has arranged a meeting with a prominent rabbi as a gesture of conciliation.

BEIRUT, SATURDAY 13
Israelis launch attacks on targets in Lebanon

Israel has launched its largest military onslaught against targets in Lebanon since 1993. Operation Grapes of Wrath is a response to rocket and mortar attacks by Iranian-backed Hizbollah guerrillas, who are targeting settlements in northern Israel from positions across the Lebanese border.

Israel's assault on Lebanon has gone beyond simple retaliation. Helicopter gunships have attacked targets in Beirut. Today, Israeli fire destroyed an ambulance, killing four children and two women. As many as 60 Lebanese are believed to have died in Israeli raids so far. (→ April 18)

CHEYENNE, WYOMING, THURSDAY 11

Child pilot killed in record attempt

Seven-year-old Jessica Dubroff in her Cessna shortly before the crash.

A seven-year-old girl may have been at the controls when a single-engine Cessna crashed today in driving rain and snow. Jessica Dubroff was killed along with her father Lloyd and her flight instructor Joe Reid.

Jessica was attempting to become the youngest person to fly across the US coast-to-coast and back. Her aircraft had just taken off from Cheyenne Municipal Airport on the second leg of the journey when it ran into trouble. It crashed into the driveway of a house in a residential area of the city. "There was a last attempt by the pilot not to hit houses," said local police chief John Powell.

A child is not allowed a pilot's licence, but an instructor can allow a child to operate the controls. Mitch Barker, an aviation administration spokesman, said Jessica would have been "considered to be a passenger; the instructor is considered in control of the aircraft".

MIAMI, FRIDAY 12

Mystery disease strikes manatees

Florida's best-loved animal, the manatee, or sea cow, is under threat. A mystery epidemic has killed 221 manatees so far this year, 120 of them in the last month. The previous record for manatee deaths was 206 in 1990. Scientists are struggling to understand the disease and save the animals – with this death rate they will be wiped out in two years. (→ July 3)

The endangered Florida manatee.

CHICAGO, WEDNESDAY 10

Tyson denies harassment allegation

LaDonna August, a beautician from Indiana, has accused boxing champion Mike Tyson of assault. Tyson is still on parole after three years in jail for rape. The alleged incident occurred at The Clique, a Chicago nightclub. According to Ms. August, Tyson touched her and bit her on the cheek. He denies the allegations.

Beautician LaDonna August.

Buenos Aires, Sunday 7. In the Argentine Grand Prix, Brazilian Formula 1 driver Pedro Diniz spins off the track with his car in flames; surprisingly, he suffered only minor injuries. The race was won by Britain's Damon Hill, who has now come first in three out of three Grands Prix this season. (→ May 5)

April

S	M	T	W	T	F	S
	1	2	3	4	5	6
7	8	9	10	11	12	13
14	15	16	17	18	19	20
21	22	23	24	25	26	27
28	29	30				

London, 14
Shadow Transport Secretary Clare Short embarrasses Labour by saying that people like herself, on middle incomes, should pay more tax.
(→ July 25)

Austria, 14
European Agriculture Commissioner Franz Fischler tells Reuters that British beef is safe to eat, but the ban must remain to calm consumer panic.
(→ April 25)

London, 14
The *Mail on Sunday* breaks a story about surrogate mother Edith Jones, aged 51, who is pregnant with her daughter and son-in-law's child.

London, 14
Sir James Goldsmith says that his Referendum party will have a £20-million budget and field 600 candidates in the next general election. (→ October 19)

Moscow, 15
Trojan gold that was seized by Soviet troops from Berlin in 1945 goes on show in Moscow amid German demands for the treasures to be returned.

East London, South Africa, 15
The Truth and Reconciliation Commission, chaired by Archbishop Tutu, opens in South Africa to look into the crimes of apartheid.

London, 16
Madonna's publicist tells GMTV that the pop star is four months pregnant; the father is Carlos Leon, a Cuban fitness instructor. (→ October 15)

Los Angeles, 17
The jury in the Menendez brothers trial recommends life imprisonment for the two young men convicted of killing their parents.

London, 17
A suspected IRA bomb explodes in the Boltons, west London. (→ April 24)

Deaths
April 13. George Mackay Brown, Scottish poet, aged 74, in Kirkwall, Orkney.

April 15. Stavros Niarchos, Greek shipping magnate, in Zurich, Switzerland, aged 86.

LAHORE, SUNDAY 14

Cancer hospital devastated by bomb blast

The hospital's founder, Imran Khan.

A bomb planted in the Shaukat Khanum cancer hospital, Lahore, killed six people today. The hospital was founded by former Pakistan test cricketer Imran Khan, now an outspoken critic of the Pakistan government. The bombing was probably politically motivated. An angry Imran Khan said:"It was the work of a savage or an animal because human beings cannot do such a thing to a hospital."

OKLAHOMA CITY, FRIDAY 19

Marking the Oklahoma tragedy

At 9:02 a.m., thousands of people stood in silence at the site of the Alfred P. Murrah federal building in Oklahoma City, where exactly one year ago a massive bomb explosion killed 168 people in the worst act of terrorism ever committed on US soil.

The 168 seconds' silence (one second for each victim) was observed by people across the US, including Congress in Washington and the New York stock exchange. Afterwards, relatives of victims came forward to leave mementos at the site.

Mourners attach mementos to the fence surrounding the federal building compound.

AUGUSTA, GEORGIA, SUNDAY 14

Norman collapse gives Masters to Faldo

Australian golfer Greg Norman, the highest-ranked player in the world, threw away a six-shot lead to lose the US Masters tournament today. After one of the most humiliating collapses in golfing history, Norman ended five strokes behind Britain's Nick Faldo.

Playing with a predatory arrogance to match his nickname, the Great White Shark had dominated the first three rounds of the tournament. He entered the last day needing only a steady performance to win easily.

But kept under constant pressure by Faldo's faultless play, Norman's confidence fell apart. The crowd was hushed as mistake followed mistake. On the final green, a comfortable winner, Faldo attempted to console a distraught Norman with a hug.

"It was an amazing day," Faldo, who had won his third Masters, said afterwards;"I honestly and genuinely feel sorry for Greg." Norman put a brave face on his disaster:"Nick played great and I played poor. There were no two ways about it."

Nick Faldo hugs Greg Norman (left) as they finish the eighteenth hole of the Masters.

LONDON, WEDNESDAY 17
Yorks divorce but stay friends

The Duke and Duchess of York were granted a "quickie" divorce in the Family Division of the High Court at Somerset House today. The couple, married in Westminster Abbey in July 1986, have been separated for more than two years. Neither was present for the granting of the divorce petition.

The Duchess said today that she and her ex-husband are still "the bestest of friends". The divorce settlement of £2 million is mostly held in trust for the children. The Duchess will have about £500,000 – not enough to cover her alleged £3 million debt. (→ May 30)

TOKYO, THURSDAY 18
US and Japan strengthen alliance

President Clinton during his trip to Japan.

In a three-day official visit to Japan, President Clinton has sought to confirm the US-Japanese alliance as the key to security in East Asia. In a joint declaration – Alliance for the 21st Century – the president pledged that US troops will stay in Asia beyond the millennium, while Japan committed itself to playing a more active role in regional defence.

The continuing presence of 47,000 US troops in Japan is highly controversial, especially since the rape of a 12-year-old Okinawan girl by three US servicemen last year. President Clinton publicly apologized for the rape in his speech to the Japanese parliament yesterday.

BEIRUT, THURSDAY 18
Israeli "mistake" is tragedy for Lebanese

A UN base near Tyre in southern Lebanon was pounded by Israeli artillery today, killing 100 people, mostly women and children. The base was crowded with Lebanese civilians who had taken refuge there to escape the Israeli bombardment of their villages. An estimated 400,000 Lebanese have fled their homes since Israel began hitting southern Lebanon eight days ago in response to rocket attacks on Israel by Hizbollah guerrillas.

The scene of carnage at the UN base was witnessed by Hassan Seklawi, a Lebanese working with the UN: "My white rubber shoes have turned red from the blood," he said. "I had to walk over bodies that covered the walkways at the base."

Israeli foreign minister Ehud Barak called the bombardment of the UN base "an unfortunate mistake". "The actual shooting was done by our forces, but the overall responsibility lies with Hizbollah and the government of Lebanon," he said. The Israelis claim they were responding to fire from Hizbollah guerrillas positioned a few hundred metres from the UN base.

Television images of the carnage have brought appeals from around the world for a halt to the fighting. US

UN paramedics carry away the wounded; 100 people were killed in the bombardment.

President Bill Clinton called for an immediate ceasefire and announced he was sending Secretary of State Warren Christopher to the region to try to further negotiations.

Israeli prime minister Shimon Peres, conscious that only a tough stance towards Israel's enemies can allow him to win the Israeli elections next month, has refused to proclaim a unilateral ceasefire. He says Operation Grapes of Wrath, the assault on Lebanon, will continue until Hizbollah agrees to stop its attacks on settlements in northern Israel. (→ April 26)

London, Wednesday 17. Plans were unveiled for a 152-m (500-ft) Ferris wheel to be built in the capital as part of the millennium celebrations. British Airways has proposed to invest £600,000 in the construction of what is being described as London's answer to the Eiffel Tower. Situated on the south bank of the Thames, the wheel would be almost twice the height of Big Ben on the opposite side of the river.

April

London, 22
Eurotunnel announces a loss of £925 million for its first year of operation.

Italy, 23
In Italian elections, the centre-left Olive Tree coalition, including the former Communist party, wins a victory over Silvio Berlusconi's right-wing Freedom Alliance.

New York, 23
Virgin chief Richard Branson rejects an accusation of sexual harassment brought by a former employee.

Moscow, 24
Reports are issued that Chechen rebel leader Dzhokhar Dudayev has been killed in a Russian missile attack.

Gaza City, 24
The PLO revises its charter, removing calls for the destruction of Israel and the expulsion of the Jews.

West London, 24
Two bombs, the biggest-ever planted by the IRA on mainland Britain, fail to explode at Hammersmith bridge.

London, 25
Jonathan Jones, jailed for murdering the parents of his girlfriend Cheryl Tooze, is freed by the Court of Appeal.

Glasgow, 25
A 15-year-old girl who "ate hamburgers excessively" is revealed as the youngest victim of mad cow disease. (→ May 14)

Lebanon, 26
Israel and Lebanon announce a cease-fire accord, in an agreement brokered by the US Secretary of State, Warren Christopher. (→ May 31)

Washington, DC, 28
President Clinton gives evidence in the Whitewater case via a protected videolink from the White House. (→ May 28)

London, 29
The House of Lords rules that a ten-year-old Zulu boy, living in Britain for four years with a white woman who wanted to adopt him, must return to his natural parents. (→ December 5)

Deaths
April 23. P.L. Travers, author of *Mary Poppins*, in London, aged 96.

Former CIA director Colby goes missing

William J. Colby, the director of the Central Intelligence Agency (CIA) from 1973 to 1976, has been missing since Sunday. His canoe was found capsized near his vacation home in Rock Point, Maryland. Coast Guard crews are searching the Wicomico River. Colby, aged 76, was the top US intelligence officer in Saigon during the Vietnam War. Currently, foul play is not suspected. (→ May 6)

Princess witnesses open-heart surgery

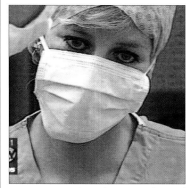

Princess Diana claimed witnessing hospital operations was a profound experience.

The Princess of Wales was filmed today observing open-heart surgery at Harefield Hospital, Middlesex. The operation, performed by Professor Sir Magdi Yacoub, took over two hours.

The princess stood with the medical team, although critics commented that she was wearing make-up and jewellery, and had hair appearing from under her theatre cap.

The patient was Arnaud Wambo, a seven-year-old boy from Cameroon. He was able to have the operation through the charity Chain of Hope, which the princess supports.

Gunman kills 34 in Tasmanian massacre

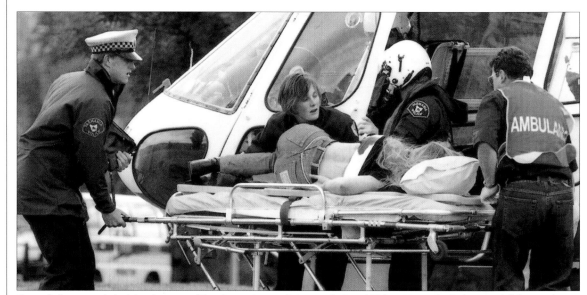

Rescue helicopters rush the injured – many of them in a serious condition – to the Royal Hobart Hospital, which was on full disaster alert.

After a siege lasting 16 hours, police this morning arrested 28-year-old Martin Bryant for the massacre of at least 34 people at Port Arthur, a popular tourist site on the Australian island of Tasmania.

The carnage began on Sunday afternoon when the gunman pulled an automatic rifle out of a tennis bag in the Broad Arrow cafeteria and opened fire at random. The cafeteria was packed with tourists, most of them Australians. Twenty people died there. Over the next 30 minutes, the gunman roamed the area, killing at will. He seized a car, shooting dead the four occupants. He pursued and killed a six-year-old girl after murdering her mother and her three-year-old sister. Finally the gunman took three hostages in the Seascape guesthouse, where he was besieged by police. Early this morning he set light to the building and ran out with his clothes on fire. Suffering from burns, he was taken to the same hospital as many of the victims he had shot.

First reports allege that Bryant has known psychological problems. It may not be the first time he has killed. His father is supposed to have shot himself, but police are now reopening the case. Helen Harvey, an elderly woman who acted as his benefactor, died in a car crash with Bryant at the wheel. (→ May 10)

Police say Martin Bryant, aged 28, has a history of psychological problems.

NEW YORK, MONDAY 29

Bidding fever for Kennedy relics

JFK's favourite rocking chair is sold for $400,000 (£270,000) – more than 300 times the pre-auction estimated price.

A bidder displays her Kennedy relic.

Asked to auction a range of Jackie Kennedy Onassis's personal possessions, Sotheby's New York estimated their overall value at $4.6 million (£3 million). The auctioneers had failed to understand America's continuing love affair with Jackie and John F. Kennedy. Today, after four days of fevered bidding, the sale had realized a grand total of $34.5 million (£20 million).

Winning bids included $400,000 (£270,000) for JFK's favourite rocking chair, estimated price $3,000 (£2,000), and $574,500 (£380,000) for the president's cigar humidor. A triple strand of fake pearls, of a kind that can be bought in department stores for around £40, sold for $211,500 (£140,000). Actor Arnold Schwarzenegger, married to a niece of JFK, paid $772,500 (£510,000) for a set of the president's golf clubs.

Jackie Onassis apparently planned the sale before her death in 1994. The proceeds will provide for the financial comfort of her children.

LOS ANGELES, WEDNESDAY 24

Superman actress in "mental distress"

Canadian actress Margot Kidder.

Margot Kidder, the Canadian actress who played Lois Lane in the *Superman* movies, is under observation in a Los Angeles hospital after being found dazed and confused in the backyard of a house in the suburb of Glendale.

Ms. Kidder, aged 47, disappeared on Saturday night from Los Angeles International Airport. When found, she appeared to have lost two teeth, had cut her own hair off with a razor, and – according to a Glendale police officer – was in "obvious mental distress". Ms. Kidder had recently been trying to make a comeback from injury and bankruptcy.

TOKYO, WEDNESDAY 24

Trial of Japanese cult leader Asahara opens

Cult leader Shoko Asahara went on trial today for ordering last year's nerve gas attack on the Tokyo underground that killed 11 and injured thousands.

Appearing before the judges in a blue prison uniform and handcuffs, Asahara refused to enter a plea and rejected the use of his real name, Chizuo Matsumoto.

Asahara's Aum Shinrikyo sect once numbered 10,000. He faces the death penalty if convicted.

LONDON, THURSDAY 25

Race killing prosecution fails

The family of Stephen Lawrence, the black teenager killed in a racist attack in south-east London in 1993, have failed in their private prosecution of three white men for the murder.

The case collapsed when the judge ruled out the identification evidence of an eyewitness as unsafe. The ruling meant the jury never saw video material, obtained by a covert police operation, showing the defendants making abusive and racist comments and brandishing knives.

The family pursued the case after the Crown Prosecution Service dropped proceedings because of insufficient evidence. Stephen's father Neville Lawrence said: "I believe in fairness. I don't think what happened today is fair at all."

LONDON, SUNDAY 21

Scottish triumph in hottest race

This year's London Marathon was the hottest and the largest ever – more than 26,000 people took part. Mexico's Dionicio Ceron was the men's winner and Scottish runner Liz McColgan won the women's competition, two years after an injury almost ended her career. McColgan is looking forward to the Olympics. "My rivals are going to have to do something extra special if I am not going to come back from Atlanta with gold," she said.

Liz McColgan celebrates her victory.

May

S	M	T	W	T	F	S
			1	2	3	4
5	6	7	8	9	10	11
12	13	14	15	16	17	18
19	20	21	22	23	24	25
26	27	28	29	30	31	

New York, 2
An agreement signed by Swiss bankers allows Jewish groups access to secret files in their search for money stolen from Jews by Nazis during the Holocaust. (→ September 14)

Madrid, 4
Jose Maria Aznar becomes the new conservative prime minster of Spain after a coalition deal is achieved.

San Marino, 5
Damon Hill wins the San Marino Grand Prix, his fourth victory out of five races this season. (→ May 19)

Moscow, 6
Russia accuses the British Embassy of running a spy ring and says it will expel several diplomats. (→ May 17)

Rock Point, Maryland, 6
Former CIA chief William Colby's body is found on a riverbank, more than a week after he disappeared while canoeing.

The Hague, 7
The Bosnian War Crimes Tribunal opens. Serbian Dusan Tadic is accused of murder, torture, and sexual violence during the "ethnic cleansing" in the former Yugoslavia 1992. (→ June 27)

Dannenberg, Germany, 8
Anti-nuclear demonstrators trying to halt the dumping of nuclear waste clash with 15,000 police in Dannenberg, north Germany.

India, 8
The corruption-racked governing Congress party is routed in Indian elections that leave no party with a clear mandate to govern. (→ May 16)

Canberra, 10
Australian politicians agree tough new firearms laws, as anti-gun sentiments sweep the country following the Tasmanian massacre. (→ September 30)

Florida, 11
A DC-9 airliner, Valujet flight 592, crashes in the Florida Everglades on its way from Miami to Atlanta. All 109 people on board the flight are believed to be dead. (→ May 16)

Wembley, 11
Manchester United win the FA Cup, beating Liverpool 1-0. Eric Cantona scores the winning goal in an otherwise uninspired match. (→ May 12)

London, Wednesday 8. A new portrait of the Queen, unveiled today, is described by the artist, Antony Williams, as "an honest painting of someone who is 70". To critic Brian Sewell, it looked like a "pensioner about to lose her bungalow".

WESTMINSTER, THURSDAY 9
Dame Shirley Porter faces £32-million bill

Tesco heiress Dame Shirley Porter faces a massive bill for alleged misconduct during her time as Conservative leader of Westminster City Council. In a 2,000-page report, district auditor John Magill accuses her and five former colleagues of running a costly scheme to keep the borough in Tory hands by selling council properties in marginal wards to probable Tory voters.

Dame Shirley and her colleagues are ordered to repay the £32 million the scheme allegedly cost. Describing the auditor's report as "blatantly unfair", Dame Shirley is appealing against the order to the High Court.

Dame Shirley Porter.

WESTMINSTER, FRIDAY 3
Tories crash in elections

Prime Minister John Major today defiantly rejected calls to resign after the Conservative party was trounced in yesterday's local elections. The Tories lost 567 seats overall, making the results among the worst ever recorded by a governing party. Their share of the total vote was 27 per cent, only 1 per cent ahead of the Liberal Democrats and 16 per cent behind Labour. The elections left 50 local councils across the country with no Conservative councillors.

The only comfort for John Major and the Conservatives was a 2-per-cent increase in the party's share of the poll over last year. Deputy Prime Minister Michael Heseltine spoke of "a small-ish, but a significant improvement".

Among councils falling to Labour were Rochdale, Oldham, and Basildon. Labour leader Tony Blair refused to see the results as a guarantee of a general election victory. "The results were excellent," he said, "but we take nothing for granted."

WESTMINSTER, TUESDAY 7
MPs fail to declare their earnings

The first attempt to make MPs reveal their earnings outside parliament – a response to the Nolan inquiry into political sleaze – has foundered in confusion and acrimony.

At least 40 MPs, most of them Tories, failed to give full details of their earnings. Many appear to have stated only a small fraction of their total income. David Mellor declared £5,000, although according to the *Guardian* he has a string of lucrative directorships. Top of the declared earnings was Roy Hattersley, with £110,000 last year from journalism.

Many MPs who did declare their earnings are said to be angry with the "fat cats" who kept quiet.

CAPE TOWN, THURSDAY 9
De Klerk deserts Mandela's coalition

F.W. de Klerk told South Africa he is "raring to go as leader of the opposition".

F.W. de Klerk announced today that his Nationalist party is to withdraw from South Africa's coalition government and go into opposition. It was the surprising alliance between de Klerk's white-supremacist Nationalists and Nelson Mandela's ANC that led South Africa out of apartheid. The break-up of the coalition seems sure to increase instability. The value of the rand fell sharply at the news, which comes a day after the South African national assembly agreed a new multiracial constitution.

CROYDON, FRIDAY 3

Fan kicked by Cantona is fined and jailed

Matthew Simmons, the football fan kicked in the chest by Manchester United star Eric Cantona in January 1995, was yesterday fined £500 for threatening behaviour. The court heard that Simmons shouted abuse at Cantona, provoking the player's assault.

After the guilty verdict, prosecutor Jeffrey McCann asked for Simmons to be banned from football grounds for a year. Simmons then lunged across the courtroom and attacked McCann. He was dragged away by police officers.

As a result of this violent incident, Simmons was further sentenced to seven days in jail for contempt. But for technical reasons he has now been released after only one day inside.

Simmons: Provoked Cantona's assault.

CORBY, WEDNESDAY 1

Girls charged over killing

Two teenage girls have been charged with the manslaughter of 13-year-old Louise Allen, who was killed in Corby, Northamptonshire, on Monday night.

Louise had apparently tried to stop a fight between other girls and was set upon herself. She was found on a verge near a funfair, with severe injuries to her head and upper torso. She died later in a Kettering hospital.

Louise was described as a friendly, good-natured girl who had never harmed anyone. (→ December 2)

Western US, May. The Olympic flame is making its way across the US from Los Angeles to Atlanta. The route was planned so that 90 per cent of the population would be able to see it without having to drive for more than two hours. On May 8 in Washington State the flame was briefly extinguished when the cyclist carrying the torch fell, but it was reignited using what organizers called the "mother flame".

MIDDLESBROUGH, SUNDAY 5

Manchester United win the title after Keegan's Newcastle falter

Manchester United won the FA Carling Premiership title in the most convincing manner today with a 3–0 victory at Middlesbrough. Kevin Keegan's Newcastle could only draw against Tottenham. On January 20, Keegan's team had led the league by 12 points, but they could not match Manchester United's consistency as the contest hotted up.

Manchester United manager Alex Ferguson said, "I feel for Newcastle, especially for their unique supporters." He may also have felt for Manchester City, relegated on the day of United's triumph. (→ May 11)

Manchester United's Alex Ferguson (left) and Newcastle's Kevin Keegan.

LONDON, THURSDAY 2

Hoddle is new England coach

After long deliberation, Chelsea manager Glenn Hoddle has accepted the job of managing England's national football team. He will take over from Terry Venables after the Euro '96 tournament this summer.

Hoddle said managing England was for him "a privilege and an honour and a burning ambition since a very young age". However, the job is widely viewed as one of the most thankless tasks in football. Many of the country's prominent coaches – Brian Robson and Kevin Keegan among them – publicly stated they would not accept the post if it was offered. Chelsea chairman Ken Bates, who tried to dissuade Hoddle from leaving his club, said: "I wish him all the luck in the world, because frankly he is going to need it."

Aged 38, Hoddle has only limited managerial experience. But he told news reporters: "I wouldn't have taken the job if I didn't feel I was ready for it in my heart."

S	M	T	W	T	F	S
			1	2	3	4
5	6	7	8	9	10	11
12	13	14	15	16	17	18
19	20	21	22	23	24	25
26	27	28	29	30	31	

Bangladesh, 13
A tornado levels 80 Bangladeshi villages, killing at least 508 people. More than 500 people are still missing.

Oxfordshire, 14
The family of a woman who died of "mad cow disease" seeks legal aid to sue the government. They allege that ministers misled the public over the safety of British beef. (→ May 21)

London, 14
President Chirac of France arrives in London by Eurostar at the start of a three-day state visit to Britain.

Oxford, 14
O. J. Simpson appears at the Oxford Union, greeted by applause. More than 1,000 members pack the debating chamber to hear him speak.

London, 15
Lisa Leeson, the wife of ex-Barings trader Nick Leeson, begins training as a Virgin Airlines flight attendant, on a salary of £8,000 a year.

London, 15
Former Archbishop of Canterbury Lord Runcie admits in a radio interview that he knowingly ordained homosexual priests.

London, 15
British writer Helen Dunmore wins the first Orange Prize for Fiction, a £30,000 literary prize exclusively for women writers.

Britain, 16
Film footage of the Beatles, taken three years before they became famous, is broadcast for the first time on television. The colour film, which has no soundtrack, was found in a drawer in a house in suburban Liverpool.

London, 17
Four Russian embassy staff are asked to leave Britain within a fortnight, in retaliation for Russia's expulsion of four British diplomats.

London, 17
Millionaire auctioneer Nicholas Bonham, a friend of the Prince of Wales, is cleared at the Old Bailey of causing death by dangerous driving.

Hampden Park, 18
Rangers win the Scottish Cup Final, beating Hearts 5-1.

Tricolour celebrations for French hero of Manchester

Thousands cheer Manchester United's triumphant progress through their home city.

Manchester United returned to their home city today after winning the FA Cup at Wembley and completing the Cup and League double for the second time.

They owed their 1-0 victory over Liverpool to an 86th-minute goal from Eric Cantona, a fitting climax to an outstanding season for the French striker, whose career last year seemed in ruins. The traditional red and black of Manchester United was overwhelmed by French tricolours as 100,000 flag-waving fans lined the streets to applaud their triumphant team and their hero, "Eric the King".

Ghana, Tuesday 14. Nearly 4,000 Liberians were granted haven here today when authorities allowed the ship Bulk Challenge to dock. In what was called "the voyage of the damned", the refugees on the ill-equipped, overcrowded ship had been seeking asylum for ten days.

Bob Dole stakes Senate seat on the presidency

Senator Bob Dole, now certain of nomination as Republican candidate for the presidency, announced today that he is to give up the Senate seat he has held for 27 years to concentrate on the presidential contest. In an emotional statement, Senator Dole said: "I will seek the presidency with nothing to fall back on but the judgement of the people, and nowhere to go but the White House or home." (→ August 15)

Washington, DC, Thursday 16. A team of palaeontologists today announced the discovery in Morocco of a skull 1.5 m (5 ft) high. The find confirms the past existence of *Carcharodontosaurus saharicus* (shark-toothed reptile from the Sahara), a carnivore bigger than *Tyrannosaurus rex*.

"Vultures" who killed young boy jailed for life

Two paedophiles who abducted, sexually assaulted, and murdered a nine-year-old boy, were sentenced to life imprisonment at the Old Bailey today. Passing sentence, the judge, Mr. Justice Curtis, described Timothy Morss and Brett Tyler as "evil vultures" and said they should never be released. Morss and Tyler first met in prison, where they shared sadistic fantasies of assaulting and killing a blond, blue-eyed boy. In 1994 they acted out their fantasy, snatching Daniel Handley from the street, abusing and strangling him.

WASHINGTON, DC, THURS.16
Top US admiral shoots himself

Admiral Jeremy Boorda, the US Chief of Naval Operations, was found dead today outside his quarters at the Washington Navy Yard. He had shot himself in the chest with a .38 pistol.

Admiral Boorda was known to be distressed by the imminent disclosure that he had improperly worn two decorations for valour to which he had no right. He described the wearing of the decorations as an honest mistake, but apparently felt that his explanation would not be believed.

NEW DELHI, THURSDAY 16
India in confusion as new PM moves in

Prime Minister Atal Bihari Vajpayee.

The collapse of the corruption-racked Congress party in last week's Indian elections has left the world's second most populous nation in a state of uncertainty and confusion. Congress had dominated Indian political life since independence.

Today, with no group commanding a majority, Atal Bihari Vajpayee, head of the Hindu Bharatiya Janata Party (BJP), was sworn in as prime minister. His chances of governing effectively look slim, however. The BJP won less than 25 per cent of the popular vote.(→ May 28)

MIAMI, THURSDAY 16
Valujet crash raises questions

The salvage site of the Valujet crash.

As investigators continue the task of searching the Everglades swamp for fragments of Valujet Flight 592, which crashed there last Saturday, a theory has begun to emerge of a cause for the disaster. About 50 oxygen canisters, officially hazardous cargo, were being carried under the aircraft's cabin. They had been wrongly labelled as empty.

Valujet's safety record, and that of other economy airlines, is coming under hostile scrutiny. President Clinton has ordered the Transportation Department "to ensure all our airlines continue to operate at the highest level of safety".

WESTMINSTER, WEDNESDAY 15
Fresh doubt cast on IRA convictions

Journalists were speculating today that up to a dozen convictions for terrorist bombing offences might be overturned because of carelessness at a government laboratory.

According to the Home Office, a centrifuge used to test for explosives in bombing cases was found to have been contaminated with minute traces of Semtex. The traces had probably been there since 1989.

Home Secretary Michael Howard described the chances that a miscarriage of justice had occurred as "very small". But he has nonetheless ordered an independent investigation of cases that might have hinged on evidence of Semtex traces found in tests at the laboratory.

Michael Howard: Maintains that chances of miscarriage of justice are small.

KATHMANDU, TUESDAY 14
Death and heroism as storm sweeps Everest

US mountaineer Seaborn Weathers, at a press conference after his rescue. He suffered severe windburn to his face, and had badly frostbitten hands.

About 30 climbers were attempting to scale Mount Everest, the world's highest peak, last weekend when a blizzard struck. One US mountaineer was rescued yesterday by helicopter, but eight other climbers are still missing, presumed dead.

The US climber, Seaborn Weathers of Dallas, Texas, was near the summit when the storm began. He struggled down the mountain for three days before being airlifted out from 6,000 m (20,000 ft). He was suffering from severe frostbite and windburn.

Less fortunate was New Zealand climber Rob Hall. On Saturday night, trapped at 7,500 m (25,000 ft) with no tent or sleeping bag, Hall made a last radio call to his pregnant wife. He is presumed to have died.

JAKARTA, THURSDAY 16
Indonesian troops free rebels' hostages

Four young Britons were among nine hostages freed when Indonesian troops attacked a rebel camp in the jungle of Irian Jaya yesterday. The four – Anna McIvor, Daniel Start, William Oates, and Annette van der Kolk – are all Cambridge science graduates in their twenties. They had been held hostage since January.

The Indonesian troops were advised by specialists from the British SAS. They found the rebel camp using heat-seeking devices and tracker dogs. Six rebels were killed in the fighting that ensued. Two hostages were killed by their captors.

The rebels belong to the Free Papua Movement, which is seeking independence for Irian Jaya from Indonesian rule. The British hostages apparently sympathized with the rebels' political cause.

S	M	T	W	T	F	S
			1	2	3	4
5	6	7	8	9	10	11
12	13	14	15	16	17	18
19	20	21	22	23	24	25
26	27	28	29	30	31	

Dartmoor, 19
More than 1,000 young walkers have to be rescued from Dartmoor by the army in appalling weather conditions.

Monaco, 19
Olivier Panis of France wins a Monaco Grand Prix in which only three cars finish. British driver Damon Hill dropped out when well in the lead. (→ June 2)

Paris, 19
France announces that Manchester United star Eric Cantona will not be part of their squad for the upcoming European Championships.

New York, 20
The UN clears the way for Iraq to recommence limited oil exports to pay for food and medicine. It is the first easing of sanctions on Iraq since the 1991 Gulf War.

London, 20
Railtrack shares soar in value after the privatization launch. The £1.93 billion sale is the government's most controversial privatization to date.

West Yorkshire, 20
WPC Karen Wade loses her sexual harassment case brought against fellow officers of West Yorkshire Police.

Taiwan, 20
President Lee Teng-hui, first popularly elected leader of Taiwan, is inaugurated. He says that he is willing to "make a journey of peace" to Beijing.

Washington, DC, 21
The House Judiciary Committee hears evidence of arson at black churches throughout the southern US – 28 cases since the start of 1995. (→ June 12)

Jordan, Montana, 22
An attempt by Colorado state senator Charles Duke to mediate a settlement with the anti-government Freemen in Montana fails. (→ June 12)

Washington, DC, 22
A study shows that there may be as many as 250,000 attacks on Pentagon computer systems each year, and 65 per cent of hackers are successful.

South Korea, 23
A North Korean air force pilot, 30-year-old Lee Chul Soo, defects to South Korea in a MiG-19 jetfighter.

LONDON, WEDNESDAY 22
Hope and tragedy of child cancer sufferers

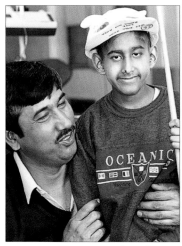

Seven-year-old Vijay Negi, shown here with his father Keshar.

A new treatment for cancer has been tried on two children in Britain, it was announced yesterday. Four-year-old Bilal of Glasgow and seven-year-old Vijay Negi of north London were recipients of cell transplants from the umbilical cords of newborn siblings. The treatment is similar in principle to a bone-marrow transplant. Only time will tell whether it is a success.

Tragically, on the same day this news emerged, Jaymee Bowen, the leukaemia sufferer whose struggle for NHS treatment as "Child B" made national headlines, lost her brave fight for survival. She died aged 11.

ALGERIA, FRIDAY 24
Killing of monks shocks France

Islamic extremists belonging to the Armed Islamic Group (GIA) have murdered seven French Trappist monks in Algeria. The monks were kidnapped two months ago in an attempt to force France to release Islamic terrorists held in its prisons.

More than 100 foreigners have been killed in Algeria since 1993. Islamic fundamentalists are trying to overthrow the Algerian government through a terror campaign. They regard France as the main backer of the government.

WESTMINSTER, TUESDAY 21
Major declares war on Europe over beef ban

Prime Minister John Major told the House of Commons today that Britain will systematically disrupt the business of the European Union in retaliation for its intransigence over British beef exports. Non-cooperation will block all measures requiring unanimity in the EU.

To cheers from anti-European Tory MPs, an angry Mr Major said: "We cannot continue business as usual within Europe when we are faced with this clear disregard by some of our partners of reason, common sense, and Britain's national interests."

The move followed the refusal of European agriculture ministers to relax the ban on the export of beef by-products or to discuss lifting the export ban on British beef. (→ May 28)

Connecticut, Monday 20. Actor Jon Pertwee died today, aged 79, while on holiday in the US. He was known to millions as *Dr. Who*, a part he played on television from 1970 to 1974. He was also famous for the children's character he played for ten years – *Worzel Gummidge*.

LIVERPOOL, WEDNESDAY 22
Millionaire Oyston jailed for rape

Owen Oyston, a prominent 62-year-old millionaire businessman, was jailed for six years at Liverpool crown court today. Oyston was found guilty of rape and of indecent assault.

The charges related to an evening five years ago, when Oyston had allegedly forced a 16-year-old model to have oral sex and then later raped her. "You were rich and powerful with a strong personality," the judge told Oyston when passing sentence. "She was young, dependent and vulnerable... I don't believe she led you on in any way."

Oyston's lawyer said after the trial that his client was "very disappointed at the result". Oyston is a flamboyant public figure, the chairman of Blackpool Football Club, and a contributor to Labour party funds. He has a wife and five children. (→ September 12)

PALERMO, TUESDAY 21
Italian police strike another blow against the mafia

Giovanni Brusca, allegedly one of the top mafia bosses in Sicily, was under arrest today, after 400 police surrounded the villa where he was hiding out. Brusca is thought to have been directly responsible for one of the mafia's most notorious crimes, the assassination of popular anti-mafia judge Giovanni Falcone in 1992.

Brusca's arrest is the latest in a series of successes for the Italian police that have put many leading mafiosi behind bars. It is also a boost for the new Italian government of Prime Minister Romano Prodi, which has promised to crack down on organized crime.

A former Christian Democrat prime minister, Giulio Andreotti, is on trial for allegedly protecting the mafia. The mafiosi no longer have enough friends in high places to save them from imprisonment.

Giovanni Brusca (right) after his arrest.

WASHINGTON, DC, TUESDAY 21
500-year-old Inca ice maiden goes on display in Washington

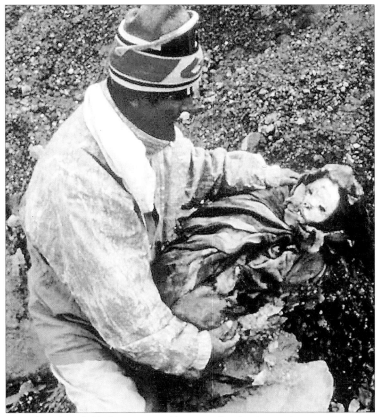

An anthropologist holds the 500-year-old mummy found on Mount Ampato in Peru.

A pubescent Inca girl sacrificed to the gods some 500 years ago went on display in Washington, DC today. Known as "Juanita", the girl was found in a tomb on the summit of Mount Ampato in the Andes last September. The girl's body had been naturally mummified by the freezing conditions on the volcanic peak.

Experts have established that she died from a blow to the head with a club, which left no external traces. She was buried in ceremonial clothes, surrounded with offerings to the gods.

SWANLEY, KENT, MONDAY 20
"Road rage" blamed in senseless motorway killings

A man who was stabbed to death on a motorway slip road yesterday is being described as the latest victim of "road rage" – an outburst of uncontrollable anger resulting from the stresses of driving.

Stephen Cameron, aged 21, was a passenger in a van driven by his fiancée Danielle Cable. As they approached the M25 at Swanley, Kent, they had to brake to avoid hitting another vehicle, a Land Rover Discovery. Shortly after this minor incident, the van and the Land Rover stopped at traffic lights. The driver of the Land Rover and Mr. Cameron got out of their vehicles and a fight started. Mr. Cameron's fiancée watched helplessly as the other driver produced a knife and stabbed her boyfriend in the chest. Mr. Cameron died in hospital. The driver of the Land Rover has not been found.

Police have attributed the attack to "a moment of madness". There has been a spate of similar incidents recently, leading one judge to speak of a "road rage epidemic". Last week, for example, a Leeds man, Paul Conlon, was convicted of running over and killing a man who was waiting for treatment after being injured in a hit-and-run accident. Conlon apparently did it because he was frustrated by the traffic jam caused by the original accident. (→ September 13)

LAKE VICTORIA, TUESDAY 21
Hundreds drowned in ferry disaster

More than 500 people are feared to have died when a ferry capsized on Lake Victoria today, 30 miles north of Mwanza, Tanzania. Many were teenagers returning to their homes at the end of the school term. Only 40 survivors were pulled out of the water alive. The disaster apparently occurred when the ship struck a rock.

The ferry, the Tanzanian-owned Bukoba, was officially authorized to carry 433 passengers, but eyewitnesses said many more were on board when the accident happened.

Cannes, Monday 20. Mike Leigh's *Secrets and Lies* **won the Palme d'Or for best picture, and the best actress for Brenda Blethyn (shown to the right of Leigh, above right) at the Cannes Film Festival. Canadian director David Cronenberg (above left) won a special prize for "audacity and daring" for his film** *Crash.*

S	M	T	W	T	F	S
			1	2	3	4
5	6	7	8	9	10	11
12	13	14	15	16	17	18
19	20	21	22	23	24	25
26	27	28	29	30	31	

Scotland, 26
Pamela Crossan swims for four hours to shore after a fishing boat capsizes in the Firth of Clyde. Four fellow crew members are drowned.

Burma, 26
Despite arrests and intimidation, the Burmese opposition, led by Daw Aung San Suu Kyi, hold a mass meeting in Rangoon.

Albania, 26
An election victory for the ruling conservatives in Albania leads to calls from the opposition party for a protest against voting irregularities.

Lord's, London, 27
Ray Illingworth, chairman of the England selectors, is told that he must face a disciplinary committee for bringing the game into disrepute in published extracts of his book. (→ June 18)

Brussels, 28
Britain vetoes 12 policy decisions in Brussels as part of its campaign against the EU beef ban. (→ June 21)

Little Rock, Arkansas, 28
Defendants in the Whitewater trial – Jim McDougal and his ex-wife Susan, and Arkansas governor Jim Guy Tucker – are found guilty, a blow for President Clinton, who testified for the defence. (→ September 10)

Stirling, 29
The inquiry into the Dunblane massacre opens. Agnes Watt, mother of killer Thomas Hamilton, is to give evidence. (→ June 7)

London, 30
An advertiser withdraws from *Vogue* because of the alleged use of excessively thin models in its June edition.

Britain, 30
The government releases figures showing that road deaths in Britain have fallen to their lowest level since records were first kept in the 1920s.

Zurich, 31
FIFA announce that Japan and South Korea will jointly host the 2002 Football World Cup.

Pennsylvania, 31
Millionaire John du Pont, on trial for the murder of Olympic wrestler Dave Schultz, claims to be the Dalai Lama.

Wife who killed abusive husband freed

Sara Thornton after her release; a retrial found her guilty of manslaughter, not murder.

Sara Thornton, the woman whose conviction for murdering her husband started a national campaign, was freed today after a retrial. A jury decided that she was guilty of manslaughter, but not of murder. She had already served five years in jail.

Sara Thornton stabbed her husband Malcolm to death while he lay in a drunken stupor. She claimed he was an alcoholic who had repeatedly threatened to kill her. The feminist group Justice for Women took up her cause, seeing her as one of many women convicted of murder when they were in effect defending themselves against abusive partners.

At a press conference after her release, Thornton was in a mood for reconciliation. She accepted the manslaughter verdict: "For me it was fair," she said; "I took a life." And she had sympathy for her late husband. "You need to see the person you loved and killed in a good light," she said. "Malcolm had a tremendous sense of humour and he was very kind."

Yeltsin announces accord with Chechens

After 17 months' fighting that has cost over 30,000 lives, the war in Chechenia may be over. Russian president Boris Yeltsin and Chechen rebel leader Zelimkhan Yandarbiyev agreed today in the Kremlin to halt hostilities at the start of next month. The Chechen rebels, some wearing battle dress, were flown into Moscow only two hours before the agreement was announced. They calculated that the Russians would keep a promise of safe conduct back to Chechenia.

The two sides made no effort to agree on the fundamental issues that divide them. The Chechen rebels are still demanding independence, while the Russians regard Chechenia as part of their national territory. But both sides need a ceasefire. The rebels have recently suffered military setbacks, while Yeltsin cannot win the presidential election next month without peace in Chechenia. (→ June 10)

Boris Yeltsin (left) meeting with Chechen rebel leader Zelimkhan Yandarbiyev (in combat fatigues, right) at the Kremlin.

BEVERLY HILLS, CALIFORNIA, FRIDAY 31
LSD guru drops out for ever

Timothy Leary, the prophet of the 1960s psychedelic revolution, has died aged 75. Leary was a Harvard psychologist before he discovered LSD and advised a generation to "tune in, turn on, drop out". The vicissitudes of his career took him to prison and a spell as a fugitive. In later years he became a proponent of the liberating effects of electronic communication. He posted updates on his losing battle with prostate cancer on the World Wide Web.

Psychedelic guru Timothy Leary.

London, Thursday 30. The Duke and Duchess of York's ten-year marriage ended today with the issue of a decree absolute in the High Court. The Duchess, pictured above with her two daughters, says she hopes to find "inner peace" as a single, working mother.

LONDON, WEDNESDAY 29
England squad accused of vandalism

With nine days to go to the opening of the Euro '96 tournament, England's soccer squad have run into a storm of criticism from the British press. The hostile coverage climaxed today with allegations that the players vandalized the aircraft that brought them back from an already controversial Far East tour. Cathay Pacific airline said last night that damage to the plane was confined to the upper business class area where the footballers were the only passengers. The incident coincided with celebrations for England star Paul Gascoigne's 29th birthday.

There had already been reports of unruly behaviour by England players in Hong Kong, contrasting unfavourably with the disciplined approach of other European teams. (→ June 3)

JERUSALEM, FRIDAY 31
Israeli election puts peace process in doubt

It was a narrow victory, but a decisive one: Benyamin Netanyahu is the new Israeli prime minister by a majority of 30,000 votes. He polled 1,501,023 votes against 1,471,566 votes for the incumbent, Shimon Peres.

Netanyahu pledged to continue the peace process. But discontent over security was a major cause for the swing against Peres' Labour party. Netanyahu's Likud alliance campaigned on a platform of getting tough with the Arabs.

Ahmed Korei, a Palestinian leader, warned: "The region will return to tension and violence, maybe wars, if the new Israeli team implements its election slogans." (→ June 10)

New Israeli prime minister Benyamin Netanyahu (right) during his election campaign.

NEW DELHI, TUESDAY 28
India changes leadership again

India's new leader H.D. Deve Gowda.

Thirteen days ago, Hindu nationalists hailed their leader, Atal Bihari Vajpayee, as Indian prime minister. But today he is out of office following his party's inability to assemble a majority, and it is the turn of the little-known H.D. Deve Gowda to govern the world's most populous democracy. He heads a coalition of left-wing and regional parties. (→ June 12)

BELFAST, FRIDAY 31
Elections show support for Sinn Fein

The elections to all-party talks in Northern Ireland have proved that Gerry Adams' Sinn Fein remains a potent force in the nationalist community. Sinn Fein received over 15 per cent of the total vote in the Province, its best ever election performance, and won 17 seats in the 110-seat forum.

Adams, who took West Belfast with 53.4 per cent of the vote, demanded that John Major should "accept the outcome of an election which he called". But the British and Irish governments confirmed that Sinn Fein representatives will not be allowed to take part in the talks unless the IRA restores its ceasefire.

The biggest single group in the forum will be the Ulster Unionists with 30 seats. (→ June 10)

June

London, 1
Labour shadow home secretary Jack Straw presents plans to introduce night-time curfews for children and young people.

Egypt, 2
Six Muslim militants are hanged for plotting to blow up a Cairo underground station.

Washington, DC, 2
Scientists at the National Oceanic and Atmospheric Administration announce that levels of ozone-depleting chemicals in the air are declining.

London, 3
Microwaves transmitted by mobile phones may cause asthma, cancer, and other diseases, according to evidence assembled from scientists for a BBC television programme.

London, 3
The England football team accepts "collective repsonsibility" for damage caused to the Cathay Pacific jumbo jet on the return flight from Hong Kong. (→ June 8)

Ukraine, 3
President Leonid Kuchman announces the completion of the removal of the last nuclear warheads from Ukraine.

London, 4
Camelot, the national lottery operator, announces first-year pre-tax profits of £77.5 million on sales of £5.2 billion.

New York, 5
The Duchess of York sells her as yet unwritten autobiography to Simon & Schuster for $1,3 million despite signing a confidentiality clause as part of her divorce settlement. (→ September 12)

London, 5
Labour leader Tony Blair admits that he smacked his children occasionally when they were small, although he has "always regretted it".

Stirling, 7
At the Dunblane massacre inquiry, former Detective Superintendent, John Millar, defends his decision to overrule Detective Sergeant Paul Hughes's recommendation five years ago that Thomas Hamilton's gun licence should be revoked. (→ July 31)

RIVER SEVERN, WEDNESDAY 5
New bridge links England and Wales

The Prince of Wales today officially opened the second Severn Crossing, a £330-million bridge linking England directly to Wales. The bridge took an Anglo-French consortium four years to build. At 5 km (3 miles), it is the longest bridge in Britain.

There are already complaints that charges are too high – £3.80 for a car and £11.50 for a lorry to cross into Wales, with the return journey free. But expected Welsh nationalist protests at the opening did not materialize.

The new Severn Crossing: a 5-km- (3-mile-) long motorway bridge across the estuary.

BELFAST, THURSDAY 6
Mitchell appointment causes row

Senator George Mitchell, President Clinton's envoy, is to chair the all-party talks on the future of Northern Ireland that open next week. The appointment was greeted with outrage by Ulster Unionists and some Conservative MPs. They believe Senator Mitchell is sympathetic to the Irish nationalists. One Conservative MP, Terry Dicks, has threatened to withdraw support from John Major's government over the issue. Major has a majority of only one in the House of Commons. (→ June 10)

CHICAGO, WEDNESDAY 5
Di takes on basketball and wins

As part of a US tour to raise £1 million for breast cancer research, Princess Diana was in Chicago today, visiting hospitals and attending a fund-raising dinner. The dinner coincided with the Chicago Bulls' opening game in the NBA playoffs.

But Princess Di proved a greater pull, with people paying up to £3,000 for a seat. Even Michael Jordan's mother, Deloris, attended. Illinois Governor Jim Edgar said the princess was "the only person I know who can push Michael Jordan from the front page".

Enthusiastic fans greet Princess Diana outside Cook County Hospital in Chicago.

FRENCH GUIANA, TUESDAY 4
Ariane 5 launch ends in disaster

The space shuttle launcher, seconds before it is exploded by controllers.

Scientists and officials of the European Space Agency were in a state of shock tonight after the Ariane 5 rocket had to be blown up on its maiden launch. The rocket's payload – four Cluster satellites – was also lost in the disaster.

Ground controllers activated the explosion 66 seconds after lift-off because the rocket had veered off course and was beginning to break up. Neither the rocket nor its payload was insured. The value of the satellites alone is reckoned at £500 million.

François Fillon, French space minister, said a second Ariane 5 launch would go ahead. "We knew the risks we ran," he added.

Football fails to match pageantry as Euro '96 opens

St. George and the dragon engage in mock battle as part of the colourful pageantry of the Euro '96 opening ceremony at Wembley stadium.

Euro '96, the biggest football tournament held in England for 30 years, opened today at Wembley stadium in a blaze of pageantry. A crowd of 76,000, paying between £25 and £75 a seat, was treated to a colourful spectacle ranging from the release of 40,000 balloons and a parade of England football heroes to a mock-medieval representation of the slaying of the dragon by St. George.

The opening match of the tournament, England against Switzerland, was an anti-climax. A tame 1-1 draw, it confirmed the opinion of most football journalists that the England side is lacking in skill, energy, and commitment. The announcement by England coach Terry Venables that the players are being given two days' rest has been derided by the press. Special criticism is reserved for Paul Gascoigne, substituted after 50 minutes. He is ridiculed as unfit and overweight. (→ June 15)

SHEFFIELD, MONDAY 3
Hillsborough award for police opens old wounds

Fourteen police officers traumatized by the Hillsborough football ground tragedy in 1989 have been awarded a total of £1.2 million in damages. The officers had gone into the pens to rescue fans who were being crushed to death. Insurers for South Yorkshire police, Sheffield Wednesday FC, and the club's engineers agreed the award out of court. The highest payments will go to officers who retired because of post-traumatic stress.

Relatives of some of the 96 football fans, mostly from Liverpool, who died at Hillsborough, reacted angrily to the award. They had been refused any payment for stress suffered watching the disaster on television, and some had received as little as £2,000 for the loss of a relative. Trevor Hicks, a spokesman for the Hillsborough families, said: "I'm gutted and I've had several families on to me who are appalled... These officers chose to be police officers. We did not choose to be victims."

PHNOM PENH, THURSDAY 6
Pol Pot reported dead

Pol Pot, leader of the Khmer Rouge.

According to reports circulating in southeast Asia, Khmer Rouge leader Pol Pot, one of this century's most notorious political figures, may be dead or dying of malaria. Pol Pot ruled Cambodia from 1975 to 1979, directing a reign of terror that may have caused the deaths of one million people. The Khmer Rouge is now fighting a vicious guerrilla war against the Cambodian government.

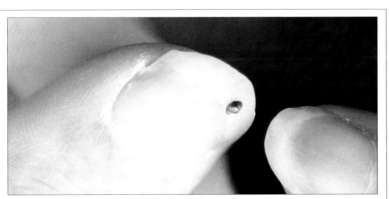

Newbury, Thursday 6. The government announced today that a colony of rare Desmoulin snails is to be moved to a new habitat away from the route of the proposed Newbury by-pass. The discovery of the 2-mm-long snails had halted the building of the road for four months.

BARCELONA, SUNDAY 2
Schumacher wins in Spanish rain

Jubilant winner, Michael Schumacher.

On a track made treacherous by rain, Michael Schumacher gave a brilliant display of driving skill to win the Spanish Grand Prix today. Only six cars finished the course. After the race, Schumacher said: "I would not have bet a penny on me winning today. I am as amazed as anybody." (→ June 16)

June

Paris, 9
Yevgeny Kafelnikov becomes the first Russian to win a major tennis title after he beats Michael Stich in five sets in the final of the French Open.

Belfast, 10
Historic all-party talks on the future of Northern Ireland begin at Stormont, east Belfast, but without Sinn Fein, excluded because of continuing IRA terrorism. (→ June 15)

Southern Lebanon, 10
Five Israeli soldiers are killed and eight are wounded in an ambush in southern Lebanon by Hizbollah guerrillas. (→ June 23)

Moscow, 10
Russian and Chechen negotiators sign a deal promising the withdrawal of all Russian troops from Chechenia by the end of August. (→ August 16)

New York, 11
British Airways and American Airlines announce an alliance to create the world's largest air network.

Washington, DC, 12
Republican Trent Lott takes over as Senate leader from Bob Dole, who bid an emotional farewell to the Senate on Tuesday.

Delhi, 12
Indian's new prime minister, H. D. Deve Gowda, wins a vote of confidence in parliament and will rule as head of the United Front coalition.

London, 12
Rock star Bob Geldof and television presenter Paula Yates agree to exchange houses as part of their divorce settlement. (→ September 26)

Jordan, Montana, 12
The anti-government Freemen group surrenders to federal agents without a struggle after an 81-day siege.

Lord's, London, 13
Women are admitted into the Lord's cricket pavilion for the first time, during a women's test match.

Florence, 14
A 40-nation conference reviewing the Dayton peace accord agrees that elections will take place in Bosnia on September 14, as planned. (→ September 18)

MANCHESTER, SATURDAY 15

IRA bomb blasts Manchester city centre, injuring 200

The Manchester bomb site – the explosion caused millions of pounds' worth of damage.

A massive IRA bomb devastated the heart of Manchester today. About 200 people were injured, nine of them seriously, including a pregnant woman expecting her baby in eight days.

After a telephone warning was received at 9:40 a.m., police identified the location of the bomb, in a parked van. They evacuated the immediate area, but when the bomb exploded at 12:40 p.m. The size of the explosion was such that shards of glass flew up to 800 m ($\frac{1}{2}$ mile) across an area crowded with Saturday shoppers.

Prime Minister John Major called the bombing "a dreadful act" and President Clinton expressed "deep outrage". It seems set to destroy the remaining credibility of Sinn Fein leader Gerry Adams in the US. (→ July 14)

More than 75,000 were evacuated from Manchester's city centre before the explosion.

Bangkok, Sunday 9. Thailand's King Bhumibol, aged 68, the world's longest-serving monarch, today celebrated 50 years on the throne with traditional pomp. As part of the Golden Jubilee celebrations, Thailand's jails will be thrown open and 26,000 prisoners released.

LONDON, FRIDAY 14

Largest-ever financial fraud revealed

Japan's Sumitomo Corporation has announced losses of around £1.2 billion in ten years' unauthorized dealing by its one-time head copper trader, Yasuo Hamanaka. The fraud is believed to be the biggest ever recorded, far exceeding the estimated £800 million losses caused by British trader Nick Leeson at Barings Bank in February last year.

Mr. Hamanaka was known as "the 5 per cent man" because he was believed to control that proportion of the world copper market. His activities were uncovered by regulators in Britain and the US. (→ October 22)

Tory MPs call for referendum on Europe

More evidence of Tory divisions over Europe was given today when 78 Tory MPs backed a bill calling for a referendum on the European Union. They included Norman Lamont, John Redwood, and Kenneth Baker.

Pro-European Tories were especially outraged that the bill's sponsor, William Cash, has accepted donations for his European Foundation from Sir James Goldsmith, leader of the Referendum party, which will oppose the Tories at the next election.

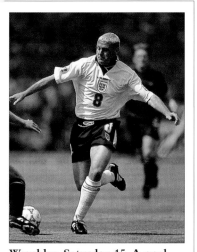

Wembley, Saturday 15. A goal of the highest quality from Paul Gascoigne clinched a 2-0 victory for England over Scotland in the Euro '96 tournament. England's other hero was goalkeeper David Seaman, who saved a penalty. (→ June 18)

Major criticizes lottery cash for gays

Prime Minister John Major today criticized awards by the National Lottery Charities Board to groups working with gays and lesbians, prostitutes, and asylum-seekers. He said they "do not in my judgement reflect the way that Parliament and public expected the lottery money to be spent." But the Board defended its decision, saying awards had been made "on the basis of merit".

Clinton denounces church burnings

President Clinton prays during a visit to the rebuilt Mount Zion church in Greeleyville.

President Bill Clinton today called on Americans of all races to unite in rebuilding black churches destroyed by arson and in resisting the divisive effects of racism. He was visiting one of more than 30 churches burned down across the southern US in the last 18 months. Standing in the car park of the new Mount Zion church in Greeleyville, South Carolina, not far from the charred remains of the old church up the road, President Clinton said: "I want to ask every citizen, as we stand on this hallowed ground together, to help rebuild our churches, to restore hope, to show the forces of hatred they cannot win."

The church-burning issue came to the forefront of national politics last weekend, when Southern church ministers lobbied Washington, and President Clinton made the church burnings the theme of his weekly radio address to the nation.

There is as yet no evidence of a conspiracy to link the acts of arson, nor are all of them believed to be necessarily an expression of racism. Few of the cases have been solved.

Not everyone was convinced by the president's call for healing and reconciliation. The Reverend Jesse Jackson, who spoke in Greeleyville before the president's arrival, denounced right-wing Republicans for encouraging a climate of racism. Jackson was supported by other black speakers.

The president refused to endorse this approach, saying that the issue of church burnings must be "kept out of politics". (→ June 20)

Jazz world mourns the loss of Ella Fitzgerald

Jazz legend Ella Fitzgerald: A self-effacing figure who set new standards for singing.

Ella Fitzgerald, jazz's "first lady of song", has died, aged 79, at her home in Beverly Hills, California. In her later years she had suffered severe health problems connected with chronic diabetes. Tragically, in 1993 both her legs had to be amputated below the knee.

Ella Fitzgerald's singing encompassed a variety of styles, but she is perhaps most famous for perfecting the technique of wordless vocal improvization known as scat. In a career that spanned 60 years, she recorded with some of the greatest names in jazz, including Louis Armstrong, Duke Ellington, and Count Basie.

Songwriter Ira Gershwin once said: "I never knew how good our songs were until I heard Ella Fitzgerald sing them." Today, famous vocalists rushed to pay tribute to her memory. Singer Tony Bennett said: "She was the lady who taught us all how to sing. She was the spirit."

June

Detroit, Michigan, 16
US golfer Steve Jones, a rank outsider, wins the US Open Championship at the Oakland Hills course.

Chicago, 16
The Chicago Bulls defeat the Seattle SuperSonics to win the NBA Championship, the top US basketball title.

Montreal, 16
Formula One driver Damon Hill wins the Canadian Grand Prix – his fifth win of the season. (→ June 30)

Westminster, 17
The unpopular Family Law Bill passes through the Commons on its third reading after the inclusion of a last-minute concession to Labour concerning the splitting of pensions between spouses on divorce.

Beijing, 17
The Chinese government agrees to crack down on copyright piracy to avert a trade war with the US.

Lord's, London, 18
The Test and County Cricket Board's disciplinary committee finds England's chairman of selectors Ray Illingworth guilty of bringing the game into disrepute through articles published in the *Daily Express*. (→ September 3)

Lord's, London, 20
Renowned cricket umpire Dickie Bird begins his last test match by giving England captain Mike Atherton out leg before wicket after five balls.

Westminster, 20
A committee of MPs clears former Treasury chief secretary Jonathan Aitken of all allegations connected with the arms-to-Iran affair.

Washington, DC, 20
President Clinton meets with the governors of southern states to discuss a response to arson attacks on black churches. Four more churches have burned since Monday, two in Mississippi, the others in North Carolina and Georgia.

Wembley, 22
England narrowly defeats Spain on penalties to progress to the semi-finals of the Euro '96 football tournament. (→ June 26)

Report accuses Hillary Clinton of abuses

WASHINGTON, DC, TUESDAY 18

In an 800-page report released today, the Republican majority on the Senate Whitewater Committee has accused Hillary Clinton of a "pattern of abuses", but has stopped short of any specific allegations of law-breaking.

The Republicans claim that Hillary Clinton was involved in all the areas they investigated, from fraudulent land deals in Arkansas to the alleged concealment of her legal billing records. Senator Alfonse D'Amato, chairing the committee, said the Clinton presidency had "misused its power, circumvented the limits on its authority and attempted to manipulate the truth".

The committee's Democrat minority strongly dissented from its critical conclusions. Their report asserts: "The American people deserve to know and now can take comfort in knowing that this year-long investigation shows no misconduct or abuse of power by their president or first lady."

England goes football crazy as the Netherlands are trounced

WEMBLEY, TUESDAY 18

Shearer drives England's third goal forcefully past Dutch goal-keeper Van der Sar.

England's football team delighted its fans by beating the Netherlands 4-1 at Wembley this evening to reach the quarter finals of Euro '96. England overwhelmed the Dutch with a sophisticated display of cultured attacking football. It was England's finest victory at Wembley since the World Cup final of 1966.

The result was not good enough to reverse Scottish fortunes. A late goal for the Dutch edged them into the next round ahead of the Scots, who beat Switzerland 1-0. (→ June 22)

New Zealand, Monday 17. Mount Ruapehu volcano, situated in the heart of North Island, has erupted, spewing out rocks and ash. The nearby town of Turangi, where residents have been advised to stay indoors, is covered with a layer of ash, and in the town of Rotorua, 129 km (80 miles) to the northeast, the touring Scottish rugby team have been forced to abandon a training session.

Russia's election too close to call

A former army officer holds the future of Russia in his hands after the closely contested first round of presidential elections last weekend. General Alexander Lebed polled under 15 per cent of the vote, but with the two main contenders – current president Boris Yeltsin and the communist challenger Gennadi Zyuganov – evenly poised for the second-round run-off on July 3, Lebed's supporters hold the balance.

Yeltsin headed the first-round poll with 35 per cent of the vote, narrowly ahead of Zyuganov on 32 per cent. Ultra-nationalist Vladimir Zhirinovsky, once tipped to succeed Yeltsin, polled only 6 per cent, a percentage point less than the reformer Grigori Yavlinsky. Former president Mikhail Gorbachev won an ignominious 0.5 per cent of votes cast.

Topping the poll was a remarkable comeback for Yeltsin, who looked unelectable only a few months ago. The energy of his performance in the campaign astonished observers who had doubted his health would survive the pressure of electioneering.

Yeltsin's supporters made full use of their control over the media and lavish financial backing. The communists were virtually barred from television during the campaign and were short of funds. (→ June 20)

Current president, Boris Yeltsin, finds new vigour as he hits the campaign trail.

Challenger, communist Gennadi Zyuganov, with supporters at a welcoming ceremony.

Yeltsin purges hardliners

As political manoeuvring continues in the wake of Sunday's first round of Russian elections, President Boris Yeltsin today announced the dismissal of the three leading hardliners in his regime, security chiefs General Alexander Korzhakov and General Mikhail Barsukov, and First Deputy Prime Minister Oleg Soskovets.

General Korzhakov was regarded as Yeltsin's closest aide and the second most powerful man in Russia. He was notoriously ruthless in his use of surveillance and police powers.

The dismissals follow the sacking of Defence Minister General Pavel Grachev on Tuesday, and the appointment of General Alexander Lebed as secretary of the security council. The elections had left Lebed as Russia's power-broker, choosing between Yeltsin and communist Gennadi Zyuganov as next Russian president. Lebed had made it clear that he favoured Yeltsin over the communist candidate. "We have gone past communism", the general said, "and have left this shore for ever."

Lebed was in a strong enough position to demand large concessions from the president in return for his support. Whether these concessions included the dismissal of Korzhakov is not yet known. (→ July 4)

Rioting French beef farmers besiege Channel ports

Protesting French beef farmers employ their cattle as placards.

As Prime Minister John Major claims victory in the beef war, a new front has opened up at Channel ports, besieged by angry French farmers. Ouistreham, near Caen, saw the worst incidents, with ferries blockaded for up to 13 hours. The farmers blame British "mad cow" disease for a sharp drop in demand for French beef.

Meanwhile, after a two-day EU summit meeting in Florence, John Major called off Britain's campaign of obstruction of EU business, claiming victory. But to many observers European concessions seemed slight. In return for a more extensive cull of British cattle, the EU agreed a stage-by-stage lifting of the beef export ban, but only at some as yet unspecified future date. (→ August 19)

Ascot, Tuesday 18. The first day of Royal Ascot brought the traditional array of spectacular millinery. Danish designer Isabell Kristensen (above) wore one of her own creations.

June

Cairo, 23
An Arab summit calls on Israel to continue withdrawing from occupied territory or endanger the peace process. The Israeli government rejects the communiqué. (→ August 28)

Northern Ireland, 25
The Prince of Wales begins a three-day visit to Northern Ireland.

Washington, DC, 26
"Filegate" hearings investigating the White House acquisition of hundreds of FBI files on Republicans begin. The White House official at the heart of the scandal, Craig Livingstone, announces his resignation.

Venice, 26
Experts investigating the Fenice opera house fire of five months ago conclude that it was started deliberately.

Kabul, Afghanistan, 26
As the former rebel leader Gulbuddin Hekmatyar is sworn in as new prime minister of Afghanistan, guerrillas assault Kabul with rockets, killing 64.

The Hague, 27
The Bosnian War Crimes Tribunal begins hearing the cases of Serb leaders Karadzic and Mladic, both accused of genocide. (→ July 11)

Wimbledon, 28
Seeded players crash in the first week of Wimbledon: Andre Agassi, Michael Chang, Jim Courier, and Monica Seles are all defeated, and Boris Becker pulls out with an injury. (→ July 3)

Washington, DC, 29
Former FBI official Gary Aldrich alleges in his book, *Unlimited Access*, that President Clinton often slips out of the White House for assignations with an unnamed female. (→ July 3)

Wembley, 30
Germany win Euro '96 with a "golden goal" in extra time against the underdog Czech Republic.

Magny-Cours, France, 30
British driver Damon Hill wins the French Grand Prix. (→ July 14)

Deaths
June 27. Albert R. "Cubby" Broccoli, US film producer best known for his Bond films, in Beverly Hills, aged 87.

BANGLADESH, MONDAY 24
New leader promises reforms

Sheikha Hasina Wajed, the new prime minister of Bangladesh who was sworn in on Sunday, has promised sweeping democratic reforms. One of the world's poorest nations, Bangladesh has had military rule for most of its 25-year existence. This year's free elections only occurred after waves of popular protest. Sheikha Hasina is the daughter of Sheikh Mujibur Rahman, who led Bangladesh to independence in 1971.

Sheikha Hasina Wajed.

LONDON, WEDNESDAY 26
Fans riot as England lose

Football fans clash with police in Trafalgar Square in rioting that led to 200 arrests.

England's hopes of winning the Euro '96 tournament were snuffed out in the cruellest manner possible in the semi-final at Wembley this evening. The home side was defeated by Germany in a penalty shoot-out after dominating most of a tense, skilful game, watched on TV by an estimated 26 million Britons.

After the match, drunken fans rioted in Trafalgar Square, battling with police and setting fire to cars. There were other disturbances across the country. (→ June 30)

ATHENS, WEDNESDAY 26
Thousands mourn a hero of Greece

Pallbearers carrying Papandreou's coffin during the pomp-filled procession through Athens.

The streets of Athens were lined with weeping crowds today as the body of Andreas Papandreou, Greece's most charismatic political leader, was carried to its last resting place. Socialist prime minister until last January, Papandreou was a prominent figure in political life in Greece for 30 years. He survived crises ranging from imprisonment after a coup in 1967 to a trial for corruption in 1991. His womanizing was legendary: seven years ago, aged 70, he married a flight attendant 36 years his junior. (→ September 12)

CAPE TOWN, SUNDAY 23
Archbishop Tutu bows out gracefully

Desmond Tutu today led a farewell service at St. George's cathedral, Cape Town, before retiring as Anglican Archbishop. During the harsh years of apartheid, Archbishop Tutu used his ecclesiastical authority to oppose white rule and to encourage South Africa on the road to democracy.

Archbishop Desmond Tutu.

Resignation after Labour U-turn on devolution

Labour leaders have announced that, if elected, they will submit plans for a Scottish parliament to a referendum. Many Labour MPs were angry at this apparent retreat from the party's policy of devolution. Jim McAllion, MP for Dundee East, resigned from the shadow cabinet today in protest. George Robertson, shadow Scottish Secretary, argued that the referendum was a change of tactics, not of policy.

Paris, Tuesday 25. British-born Christiane Amanpour becomes the world's highest paid foreign correspondent after signing a deal with both CNN and CBS for $2 million a year.

Crime journalist murdered

Veronica Guerin, a journalist who specialized in exposés of Ireland's criminal underworld, was shot dead in Dublin today. A motorbike pulled up alongside her car at traffic lights and the pillion passenger opened fire with a handgun. Police believe it was a contract killing.

Ms. Guerin, who was married with a seven-year-old child, had pursued her investigations of Dublin gang bosses in the face of extreme intimidation. In 1994 she was shot in the leg by an intruder in her home. "I just would not give in to them," she said.

Truck bomb kills 19 US servicemen

At an emotional memorial service held in Dhahran on Friday, US airmen remember 19 comrades killed in the bomb attack.

The bomb-blasted apartment building where US and other foreign servicemen were housed.

Nineteen US airmen have been killed in a truck bomb attack on an apartment building in Saudi Arabia. The men were among the 2,900 US servicemen stationed at the King Abdul Aziz Air Base near Dhahran.

The 1,350 kg (3,000 lb) bomb was left in a car-park just outside the perimeter fence of the US military compound. It devastated the men's quarters, which also housed British and French military personnel. As well as killing 19, the blast injured more than 160 people.

Although no group has yet admitted responsibility for the bomb attack, it is believed to be the work of Saudi militants hostile to the US presence in their country and to the rule of the Saudi royal family. The attack may be a direct response to the execution of four Saudis on May 31.

The US has flown in 40 FBI anti-terrorist specialists to investigate the attack. Promising to punish the terrorists who are responsible for the bombing, President Bill Clinton said: "Anyone who attacks one American attacks every American, and we protect and defend our own."

ENGLAND, JUNE 1996

England enjoys a summer festival of football

THE ENGLISH national team was absent from the European football championship final played at Wembley on 30 June. The winners were England's old rivals Germany, who defeated rank outsiders the Czech Republic in extra time. But nothing could quite dampen the party atmosphere that had taken a grip on England during the three weeks of Euro '96, the first international soccer championship staged in England since the World Cup 30 years ago.

Football comes home

Despite fears of hooliganism, the polyglot fans fraternized on the terraces in a good-natured atmosphere. And faced with the willingness of referees to brandish red and yellow cards at the slightest provocation, the players also were mostly on their best behaviour.

But what most lifted the spirits was the performance of the British participants, Scotland and, above all, the English hosts. Branded as drunks and idlers before the tournament by the British press, the England team became popular heroes after defeating Scotland very narrowly and the Netherlands by an almost unprecedented 4–1 margin.

A quarter-final win against Spain brought England up against Germany in the semi-final, a rematch of the 1966 World Cup final. A game of extraordinary tension ended with Germany winning in a penalty shoot-out.

Holding on to pride

English fans ran riot in Trafalgar Square after the defeat, burning cars and fighting with police. But nothing could alter the impression that England had had a great summer party. Even Gareth Southgate, who missed the crucial penalty against Germany, received more sympathy than ire from fans.

Prime Minister John Major was doubtless waiting to see if the country would wake up with a hangover, or would have rediscovered the "feel-good factor" that all pundits agree alone could save the Conservative government from defeat in the next general election.

Tournament features: Red and yellow cards were as plentiful as "golden goals" were scarce.

Paul Gascoigne's superb performance in the tournament silenced his critics.

Gareth Southgate walks away from the goal after his penalty miss against Germany.

France's Christian Karembeu.

Scotland only narrowly failed to qualify for the second round of the tournament.

The fans play their part in the spectacle

England goalkeeper David Seaman became a national hero after saving two "sudden death" penalties by Spain in the quarter-finals.

Vindicated: Stuart Pearce scores his penalty.

Jürgen Klinsmann (centre) and his German teammates hold up the championship trophy.

Danish supporters quickly got into the party spirit of Euro '96.

The Scottish brigade saw their team fall 2-0 to rivals England.

Croatia's tournament debut was cheered on by colourful fans.

Jubilant England fans during the quarter-final against Spain.

July

S	M	T	W	T	F	S
	1	2	3	4	5	6
7	8	9	10	11	12	13
14	15	16	17	18	19	20
21	22	23	24	25	26	27
28	29	30	31			

Northern Territory, Australia 1
The world's first law permitting euthanasia comes into force here today; it is being contested in the courts. (→ September 25)

Ulan Bator, Mongolia, 1
The Democratic Union wins a landslide in Mongolian elections, ending 75 years of control by the communists.

Thiepval, France 1
First World War veterans gather to commemorate the eightieth anniversary of the first offensive of the Battle of the Somme.

Britain, 1
A written exam is introduced for the first time as part of the driving test.

Hertfordshire, 3
England footballer Paul Gascoigne marries Sheryl Failes in a ceremony covered exclusively by *Hello* magazine.

London, 3
John Major announces that the Stone of Scone, the symbol of Scottish nationhood that Edward I carried off in 1296, is to be returned to Scotland. (→ November 15)

New York, 3
Newsweek reports that recent allegations that President Clinton slips out of the White House regularly for romantic trysts are based on a rumour that was passed on by a conservative journalist.

St. Petersburg, Florida, 3
Researchers claim to have found the cause of death of 158 manatees so far this year, blaming "red tide", a toxic build-up of natural organisms off the Florida coast.

Colombo, Sri Lanka, 4
A Tamil suicide bomber throws herself in front of a government motorcade, killing 21 soldiers and civilians.

Wimbledon, 6
Steffi Graff wins the women's singles title at Wimbledon, defeating her opponent, Arantxa Sanchez Vicario 6–3, 7–5 in 88 minutes. (→ July 7)

Deaths
July 1. Alfred Marks, OBE, comedian, actor, and singer, aged 75.

July 4. Clay Jones of BBC Radio's *Gardener's Question Time*, aged 75.

Santa Monica, Monday 1
Actress Margaux Hemingway is found dead

Margaux Hemingway, the 41-year-old granddaughter of novelist Ernest Hemingway, was found dead today in her apartment in Santa Monica. Investigators believe that she died of natural causes. Once a Hollywood star and the best-paid model in the world, Ms. Hemingway struggled in recent years with alcoholism, bulimia, and epilepsy brought on by drinking. An autopsy is scheduled for Wednesday.

Hemingway: Cause of death is unknown.

Westminster, Thursday 4
On the road to the election

Although there is as yet no general election in sight, both Labour and the Conservatives are behaving this week as if the campaign has begun.

On Tuesday the Tories launched a new attempt to frighten voters back into their fold under the slogan, "New Labour, New Danger". They began, somewhat bizarrely, with a spoof Labour manifesto, *The Road to Ruin*, from which excerpts were read out at a news conference by deputy prime minister Michael Heseltine and party chairman Brian Mawhinney as an unlikely comedy double-act.

Today Labour released their pre-manifesto statement, *Road to the Manifesto*, a much shorter document than the Tory spoof, setting out their promises for the future. These include cutting NHS bureaucracy and using the money to reduce waiting lists; a "windfall" tax on privatized utilities; and controls over public spending.

Wimbledon, Wednesday 3
Music takes over on Centre Court

Sir Cliff Richard with "backing vocalists" Martina Navratilova (left) and Gigi Fernandez.

Wimbledon lost many of its stars too early this year, with crowd pullers like Andre Agassi and Boris Becker out in the first week. But two Englishmen have enlivened a rather flat tournament. One is Tim Henman, the first British tennis player to reach the quarter-finals at Wimbledon for 23 years – in fact, since before 21-year-old Henman was born. The other is ageing pop star Sir Cliff Richard, who today treated the rainsoaked spectators in Centre Court to an impromptu concert from the royal box – with a line-up of female tennis stars as a backing chorus. (→ July 6)

Britain, Saturday 6. The bra advertisement that elicited a record 800 complaints was approved by the Advertising Standards Authority, who deemed that the outcry was "orchestrated in part by the press".

JERUSALEM, MONDAY 1
Ex-nanny knocks Netanyahu's wife

Israel's new prime minister Benjamin Netanyahu came under attack from an unexpected direction today when his family's ex-nanny denounced his wife on Israeli army radio.

The nanny, Tanya Shaw, claimed that Israel's first lady flew into a rage and threw her out on the street after a row about burnt soup. Ms. Shaw painted a grim picture of the family's life, describing Mrs. Netanyahu as unstable and obsessed with cleanliness.

The official reason given for the nanny's dismissal was that she posed a security threat. A statement described Ms. Shaw as disturbed and prone to "outbursts of violence".

Cape Canaveral, Tuesday 2. Lockheed Martin today unveiled plans for the X-33, a $1-billion wedge-shaped rocket ship that it will develop for NASA to replace the ageing space shuttle fleet by 2012.

MOSCOW, THURSDAY 4
Yeltsin wins, but fitness still in doubt

Boris Yeltsin doing the twist with a Russian pop group – his re-election campaign was filled with similar displays of youthful energy.

Boris Yeltsin has succeeded in his campaign for re-election as president of Russia. In the second round of voting, completed yesterday, Yeltsin received 53.7 per cent of the vote, as against 40.4 per cent for his communist opponent Gennadi Zyuganov.

The president adopted a conciliatory tone in his time of triumph. "Let us not divide the country into victors and vanquished," he said. The loser was less moderate. Zyuganov told reporters that if economic and social conditions continued to deteriorate,

he would "not rule out the possibility of mass riots".

Most observers, however, felt that Yeltsin was less threatened by the possible deterioration of the Russian economy than by the deterioration of his own health. Determined to demonstrate his fitness to rule, the president put on some startling displays of youthful energy during the long election campaign. But it is still doubtful whether his health will hold up through a full four-year term in office. (→ August 9)

Yeltsin seizes another dancing opportunity.

LONDON, FRIDAY 5
Diana receives Charles's terms for divorce

Princess Diana at a recent charity event.

The Prince of Wales's lawyers last night presented Princess Diana with his terms for a divorce settlement, ending a ten-week deadlock that has stalled progress towards ending their 15-year-old marriage.

Although the terms have not been made public, there is press speculation that the settlement will cost the Prince around £20 million. (→ July 12)

LONDON, WEDNESDAY 3
Mediterranean future for England

The environment secretary, John Gummer, today endorsed predictions of global warming, saying that by the year 2050 southern England would have the hot, dry climate now associated with the south of France. Although sun-worshippers may look forward to the change, Mr. Gummer stressed the negative consequences of global warming, including a rise in the sea level that will threaten low-lying areas. Britain is to press for measures to slow climate change at talks in Geneva next week.

July

Cape Canaveral, 7
The space shuttle Columbia returns to Earth after the longest ever shuttle flight, 16 days and 22 hours.

Wimbledon, 7
Dutch tennis player Richard Krajicek wins the Wimbledon men's singles final, defeating MaliVai Washington of the US in straight sets.

Wolverhampton, 8
A man armed with a machete attacks a group of children enjoying a teddy bear's picnic at St. Luke's Infants' School. Three children and four adults are seriously injured. Horrett Campbell is arrested for the attack. (→ December 4)

Trent Bridge, 9
England's cricketers hold India to a draw in the Third Test to take the series by a single win.

Newport, 10
A South Korean company, the LG Group, signs a £1.7-billion deal to build a silicon-chip plant at Newport in South Wales.

The Hague, 11
The War Crimes Tribunal issues international warrants for the arrest of the Bosnian Serb leaders General Ratko Mladic and Radovan Karadzic. (→ July 19)

London, 12
The Prince and Princess of Wales agree terms for divorce. The financial settlement is worth £15 million. (→ July 15)

Westminster, 12
After the Communication Workers' Union says it intends to go ahead with a series of one-day stoppages, the government announces that it is to end the Post Office's monopoly on carrying letters priced under £1.

London, 13
England are formally thrown out of the rugby union Five Nations Championship after making a separate TV deal with Sky.

Lord's, London, 13
Lancashire win the one-day cricket Benson & Hedges Cup by 31 runs from Northamptonshire.

Violence flares on the streets of Ulster

Catholics riot in protest across the province: In Londonderry masked men and boys throw Molotov cocktails at abandoned cars and buildings.

The Northern Ireland peace process appears to be in ruins after the worst rioting in the province for many years. The trouble began on Sunday when RUC Chief Constable Sir Hugh Annesley banned Protestant Orangemen from marching through a Catholic area in Drumcree, near Portadown. As Loyalists confronted police at Drumcree, Protestants took to the streets across the province, blockading roads and driving many Catholics from their homes.

On Thursday, faced with threats of even worse violence, the RUC let the Drumcree march go ahead. The unsurprising result of this U-turn was widespread rioting by Catholics, outraged at what they saw as capitulation to the Loyalists. (→ July 14)

Police protect the Orangemen's parade.

Mandela wins the heart of London crowds

The Queen and President Mandela ride in open-carriage procession down the Mall.

Nelson Mandela, the president of South Africa, today completed a memorable state visit to Britain. Over four days, the hero of the struggle against apartheid was hailed by the Queen as the saviour of his country, given a standing ovation by the combined Houses of Parliament, and was mobbed by adoring crowds wherever he appeared.

On the final day of his visit Mandela went on a walkabout in Brixton and ended by making a speech from the balcony of the South African embassy in Trafalgar Square. "I wish I had big pockets," he told the crowd; "I would take each and every one of you and put you in my pocket and take you back to South Africa."

CANTERBURY, THURSDAY 11
Mother and child killed in "frenzied" attack

Lin, Megan, Shaun, and Josephine Russell.

A mother and daughter were bludgeoned to death in a quiet country lane in Kent this afternoon. Lin Russell and her daughters Megan, aged six, and Josephine, aged nine, were walking home from Goodnestone Primary School when they were attacked. Josephine survived, although she is seriously injured.

Detective Chief Inspector David Stevens described the attack as "utterly frenzied". He said it was unlikely Josephine would be able to identify the killer, because of the scale of her injuries. (→ September 10)

WESTMINSTER, WEDNESDAY 10
Politicians vote for more money

MPs tonight ignored the views of the electorate and of their party leaders by voting themselves a massive pay rise. The increase of 26 per cent, backdated to July 1, will give MPs a salary of £43,000 a year. Cabinet ministers see their pay increase to £86,991 a year, while the prime minister will now have a salary of £101,557.

Opinion polls in recent days have shown three out of four electors opposed to a steep increase in MPs' pay. The leaders of the three main parties all recommended a rise of 3 per cent. But MPs for once followed their own judgement rather than the party line or electoral calculation. The majority for the rise was 125.

In future MPs will be spared the embarrassment of voting on their own pay. Rises will be linked to those of senior civil servants.

PARIS, TUESDAY 9
The autumn look is luxuriant and ultra slender

The twin notes of this week's autumn haute couture shows are luxury and sleekness. Gianfranco Ferre, presenting his final collection for Dior, offered opulent, shimmering, Indian-inspired gowns for the curvaceous, as well as tailored suits for the tall and slender. Karl Lagerfeld, at Chanel, emphasized thinness by using body-stockings beneath long satin gowns and Chinese-embroidered coats.

Claudia Schiffer for Yves Saint Laurent.

Nadia Auermann models for Lacroix.

Linda Evangelista models for Lacroix.

Karl Lagerfeld (centre) employs the new breed of ultra-thin supermodel to reinterpret the flapper-girl look for Chanel.

July

NEW YORK, FRIDAY 19

Terrorism suspected in TWA disaster

The recovery crew pulls wreckage out of the sea at the crash site off the Long Island coast.

Investigators are still searching today for a clue to the catastrophe that struck TWA Flight 800 two days ago. The Boeing 747 jumbo jet exploded at 8:45 p.m. on July 17 shortly after taking off from New York's JFK International Airport. Many witnesses saw the burning fragments of the aircraft plunge into the Atlantic off Long Island. There are no survivors.

The TWA flight was bound for Paris with 228 people on board – 210 passengers and 18 crew. Among those killed were a party of 16 high-school students from Montoursville, Pennsylvania, accompanied by three adults. The mayor of Montoursville, John Dori, commented: "The whole town is in mourning."

Sonar equipment has located wreckage more than 36 m (120 ft) below the surface off the coast of Long Island, but the search for evidence is being hampered by fog, wind, and choppy seas. More than 100 bodies have been retrieved. Divers are preparing to search for the flight recorders, which may throw light on the cause of the tragedy.

Investigators have identified three possible causes for the devastating explosion – a bomb, a missile, or mechanical failure. The most likely explanation is a terrorist bomb planted on board. But some eyewitnesses claim to have seen a streak of light heading towards the plane, suggesting a missile attack. Alternatively, an engine fault might have ignited the plane's fuel tanks. The Boeing 747 has, however, a superlative track record for mechanical safety.

President Clinton yesterday advised against speculation on possible terrorist involvement. "Let's wait until we get the facts and let's remember the families," he said. (→ July 25)

New Jersey, Sunday 14. The latest attempt to market professional soccer in the US seems to be working. The Major Soccer League's first All-Star Game drew 78,416 spectators to the Giants Stadium. Homegrown US players such as Alexi Lalas (far right) mix with imports such as Carlos Valderrama of Colombia (third from right).

WASHINGTON, DC, WED. 17

Primary suspect finally owns up

Primary Colors author Joe Klein.

The "Anonymous" author of the best-selling political satire *Primary Colors* was revealed today as *Newsweek* columnist Joe Klein. Always a prime suspect, Klein once said: "For God's sake, definitely, I didn't write it." Now, trapped by a handwriting expert hired by the *Washington Post*, he has owned up. The book has already sold more than a million copies.

ATLANTA, GEORGIA, FRIDAY 19

Olympics open with pomp and emotion

A highlight of the opening ceremony – a giant light show with blown-up silhouettes of athletes in classical Grecian-style poses.

Muhammad Ali's lighting of the Olympic torch was the emotional climax of the opening.

The Centennial Olympics opened in Atlanta, Georgia, this evening with a ceremony second to none in the history of the games.

Some 11,000 athletes from 197 nations, plus 8,000 other performers, contributed to the overwhelming spectacle - as well as around 5,000 fireworks and a fleet of chrome trucks. High points included Gladys Knight singing, "Georgia On My Mind" and a recording of a speech by Atlanta's most famous son, Martin Luther King Jr. At one stage, massive silhouettes of athletes were projected on to a screen like a Grecian frieze.

But if the opening ceremony astonished with its sheer size, it was the courage of a single individual that provided the most unforgettable moment of the evening. Muhammad Ali, once the greatest boxer in the world, proudly overcame the ravages of Parkinson's disease to light the Olympic flame. To many, he seemed to represent the true spirit of the Olympic dream. (→ July 27)

BRITTANY, SATURDAY 20

Girl murdered on school trip

French police are searching for the killer of Caroline Dickinson, a 13-year-old British schoolgirl who was raped and murdered on a school trip in Brittany. She was found dead in her bed this morning in the hostel room she was sharing with four girls.

Police are questioning the other 39 children in the school party from Launceston College in Cornwall, and are investigating the possibility that Caroline was killed by a prowler – one girl reportedly heard footsteps outside at 4:00 a.m. The school's headmaster has described his pupils as "devastated" by the event. (→ July 22)

Thirteen-year-old Caroline Dickinson.

Los Angeles, Thursday 18. US basketball star Shaquille O'Neal signs a $120 million (£80 million), seven-year deal with the LA Lakers to become one of the world's highest paid sportsmen.

ENNISKILLEN, NORTHERN IRELAND, SUNDAY 14

Hotel bombing crowns a week of renewed violence

In the early hours of this morning, Northern Ireland suffered its first terrorist bombing for two years. It is the culmination of a week of mounting sectarian violence.

A Catholic couple were holding their wedding celebration at the Killyhevlin Hotel in Enniskillen, County Fermanagh, when a telephone warning was received at 11:40 p.m. The last guests had just cleared the building when a 545 kg (1,200 lb) bomb exploded. It devastated the hotel and destroyed more than 20 cars. Forty people were taken to hospital, most with minor injuries.

The IRA denied carrying out the bombing; a breakaway Republican group is suspected. There are fears that loyalists might respond by ending their own ceasefire.

S	M	T	W	T	F	S
	1	2	3	4	5	6
7	8	9	10	11	12	13
14	15	16	17	18	19	20
21	22	23	24	25	26	27
28	29	30	31			

Paris, 21
Bjarne Riis of Denmark wins the Tour de France cycle race.

Paris, 22
French police arrest a vagrant, Patrice Pade, for the murder of British school-girl Caroline Dickinson. (→ August 6)

London, 23
Treasury minister and Eurosceptic David Heathcoat-Amory resigns from the government in opposition to its European policy.

London, 23
Lightning hits three guests at a garden party at Buckingham Palace. The Queen, who was 135 m (150 yd) away, is unhurt.

London, 23
Princess Diana's public relations aide, Jane Atkinson, resigns six months before the end of her contract.

London, 24
Buckingham Palace announces that the Queen's Christmas broadcast will cease to be a BBC exclusive – apparently in retribution for *Panorama*'s interview with Princess Diana last year.

Bujumbura, Burundi, 25
An army coup deposes the president of Burundi, Sylvestre Ntibantunganya, arousing fears of new massacres in central Africa. (→ July 31)

Luton, 25
British Midland airline is ordered to pay £175,000 in fines and costs for putting passengers at risk through a dangerous leakage of engine oil.

London, 26
Home Secretary Michael Howard refers the case of the 1978 murder of newsboy Carl Bridgewater to the Court of Appeal for the second time.

Jakarta, Indonesia, 27
Violent demonstrations rock Jakarta as protesters challenge the 30-year rule of President Suharto. (→ July 30)

Sydney, 27
Ivan Milat is jailed for life for the murder of seven backpackers in Australia.

Deaths
July 20. Lieutenant-Colonel Colin Mitchell ("Mad Mitch"), soldier and politician, aged 70.

NEW YORK, THURSDAY 25
New clues found in TWA crash investigation

Analysis of the cockpit voice recording from TWA Flight 800 has revealed the presence of a brief noise immediately before the tape ended and the aircraft crashed. The recovery yesterday of the voice recorder and the flight data recorder – the so-called black boxes – is providing aviation experts with new leads in attempting to solve the mystery of TWA Flight 800's sudden disappearance off the coast of Long Island.

A similar noise was heard on Pam Am Flight 103, shortly before it was blown out of the sky by a bomb in December 1988 while flying over Lockerbie in Scotland. This, and the absence of any vocal warning on the flight recorder, reinforces the theory that a bomb is responsible for the downing of TWA Flight 800.

President Clinton has announced wide-ranging measures to increase aircraft security, acknowledging that while they would increase expense and inconvenience, "the safety and security of the American people must be our first priority". (→ July 30)

SOUTHEAST CHINA, TUESDAY 23
China mobilizes to hold back river

In a desperate attempt to hold back the waters of the flooded Yangtze river, hundreds of thousands of soldiers and workers are being mobilized to plug leaks in embankments. Rainfall of unusual severity has caused flooding in nine provinces, killing more than 850 people.

Holding back the Yangtze has become a national priority, with more than 600,000 people deployed to watch for cracks in the dykes and to fill holes made by snakes and rats. An official at Flood Control Headquarters in the city of Wuhan said: "We are guarding the banks with our lives. This is a critical moment."

The US is leading an international relief programme to provide aid to the stricken provinces. Water purifiers, plastic sheeting, and blankets are being sent to the flooded regions.

Aid workers from the Red Cross deliver medicine to flood victims in Hubei province.

JAKARTA, INDONESIA, SUNDAY 21
Jackson makes human rights appeal

Jesse Jackson: Fighting for workers' rights.

US politician Jesse Jackson is touring Indonesia to dramatize complaints of abuses by US-owned companies. During his visit, Jackson met Indonesian pro-democracy leader Megawati Sukarnoputri, and both declared themselves allies in the battle to protect the rights of workers in Third World countries. Jackson preached two sermons in Jakarta churches, and said: "The rich are exploiting the poor, but the Christian must defend the poor."

LONDON, THURSDAY 25
Short a casualty in Labour reshuffle

Clare Short was sacked from her post as shadow transport secretary by Labour leader Tony Blair in the latest reshuffle of his shadow cabinet. Reluctantly, she has been persuaded to accept a low-key role in overseas development. Short has repeatedly embarrassed the Labour leadership with well publicized calls for the legalization of cannabis and increased levels of taxation for those with middle incomes and above. (→ August 7)

New York, Monday 22. Rhett Butler may have said, "Frankly my dear, I don't give a damn", but *New York* magazine has named *Gone with the Wind* the most commercially successful film in the history of motion pictures. Second place goes to the musical, *The Sound of Music*.

ATLANTA, GEORGIA, SATURDAY 27

Terrorist bomb blast rocks Atlanta, leaving two dead

Police disperse the crowd in the wake of the bomb blast in Centennial Park.

Paramedics administer first aid to victims of the bombing. One person was killed outright, another subsequently died of a heart attack.

The harmony of the Olympic Games has been devastated by an explosion during a concert in the Centennial Olympic Park at 1:25 a.m. today. The bomb, which was placed near a sound tower, left two people dead, and injured a further 111. A warning call was made 18 minutes before the blast, and officials say the caller's voice had the characteristics of a white US male. This has led the FBI to believe the explosion was the result of domestic terrorism

Security at the Games has been stepped up, and an army of state and federal agents are searching for clues to track down those responsible for the outrage. (→ July 30)

ATLANTA, GEORGIA, SATURDAY 27

US golden girl breaks through pain barrier at Olympics

Despite badly spraining her ankle, US gymnast Kerri Strug battled on to help the US women's team win gold on Wednesday, ending years of Russian dominance in this event. The contest was watched by millions, ensuring Strug's position in the pantheon of US sporting heroes.

Irish swimmer Michelle Smith dominated in the pool, gaining three golds and a bronze, while earning the enmity of an envious US swimming establishment, which repeatedly made innuendos associating Smith with drug taking. For Britain, Steven Redgrave won his fourth gold medal in four successive Olympics, when he and his partner Matthew Pinsent won the coxless pairs. But Linford Christie failed in his bid for gold in the men's 100 m, victory going to Canada's Donovan Bailey. Christie was disqualified from the race for two false starts. (→ July 31)

Kerri Strug is carried to the medal ceremony by the US gymnastics coach, Bela Karolyi.

SRI LANKA, WEDNESDAY 24

Tamil Tigers unleash new offensive

Resurgent Tamil Tigers have blown up a crowded commuter train outside Sri Lanka's capital, Colombo, killing more than 60 people and wounding nearly 450 others. The attack was part of a new terrorist campaign instigated by the Tigers to reassert their authority over the Jaffna peninsula, following their expulsion by government forces last year.

Yesterday, a government army camp was overrun by the Tigers after a ferocious mortar bombardment. According to rebel sources, only a handful of troops escaped, out of a garrison of over 1,200. Although government forces have now recaptured the camp at Mullaitivu, the Tamil Tigers have proved their ability to mount conventional operations.

S	M	T	W	T	F	S
	1	2	3	4	5	6
7	8	9	10	11	12	13
14	15	16	17	18	19	20
21	22	23	24	25	26	27
28	29	30	31			

Hockenheim, Germany, 28
British driver Damon Hill wins the German Grand Prix – his seventh victory of the season, giving him a 21-point lead in the Formula One drivers' championship. (→ August 11)

Norwich, 29
Police driving instructor Gerard Sharrat, who killed nurse Judith Hood in a car crash while engaging in a mock chase, is given a £750 fine.

Atlanta, 29
US sprinter Michael Johnson wins the men's 400-m race at the Atlanta Olympics. Roger Black wins the silver medal for Britain. (→ July 31)

Liverpool, 30
A jury clears three women who vandalized a Hawk fighter jet destined for Indonesia, causing £1.5 million in damage. The women said their actions were justified on political grounds.

Jakarta, Indonesia, 30
The Indonesian military threatens to shoot rioters on sight amid rumours of fresh disturbances in the capital.

London, 30
The Court of Appeal rules that the Home Secretary, Michael Howard, acted unfairly when he set a minimum 15-year sentence for the two boys who murdered two-year-old James Bulger.

New York, 30
Jim Kallstrom, the FBI agent in charge of the TWA Flight 800 crash inquiry, admits that there is still no hard evidence that the plane was brought down by a bomb. (→ October 12)

Moscow, 30
Pravda, the newspaper founded by Lenin 84 years ago, bows to market forces and is relaunched as a down-market tabloid.

Westminster, 31
Six Conservative MPs on the Commons Home Affairs Select Committee oppose a ban on private handgun ownership in the wake of the Dunblane massacre. (→ September 11)

Arusha, Tanzania, 31
African leaders agree to impose a total economic blockade on Burundi after last week's coup, to press for a return to constitutional rule. (→ August 6)

ATLANTA, GEORGIA, TUESDAY 30
Bombing hero becomes a suspect

Richard Jewell, the 33-year-old security guard who was credited with spotting the bomb.

Richard Jewell, the security guard hailed as a hero in the Centennial Olympic Park bombing, is being questioned by the FBI. Officials say that Jewell, who was credited with spotting the bomb, may have planted the device in order to set himself up as a hero. Jewell made several TV appearances following the bombing, but video footage from surveillance cameras in the park contradicts some of his statements. (→ August 5)

Barbados, Tuesday 30. Claudette Colbert, star of more than 60 films, dies aged 93. She won an Academy Award in 1934 for her starring role alongside Clark Gable in *It Happened One Night*.

PARIS, TUESDAY 30
Leading powers target terrorism

The world's leading political powers met in Paris today to agree measures for combating terrorism. A wave of terrorist attacks around the world, most recently in Atlanta and Dhahran, prompted the one-day meeting for the seven leading industrial nations and Russia. The group's recommendations include tightening border checks, simplifying extradition rules, and investigating charitable groups thought to back terrorists.

NEWCASTLE, MONDAY 29
Shearer scores £15-million deal

England striker Alan Shearer today signed a deal to move from Blackburn to Newcastle United for £15 million, making him the most expensive football player in the world. The sum is £2 million more than the previous world-record transfer fee.

The star of Euro '96 was widely expected to go to Manchester United, but Newcastle outbid them by £3 million. "I just love signing big players and there is none bigger than this one," said Kevin Keegan, manager of Newcastle United, after his coup.

England's top scorer in Euro '96, Alan Shearer (left), with a delighted Kevin Keegan.

LONDON, WEDNESDAY 31

Ian Botham "astonished" by libel case defeat

Former England cricketer Ian Botham, after losing his libel case against Imran Khan.

Cricket celebrities Ian Botham and Allan Lamb face a £400,000 legal bill, after losing their libel case against former Pakistan captain Imran Khan. In a 13-day trial that featured a dozen England cricketers giving evidence along with lengthy discussions on ball tampering, Botham and Lamb sought to prove that Imran had accused them of cheating and racism in two separate newspaper interviews.

"I am overjoyed," said Imran, who, although he faces his own £100,000 legal bill, said he would have been bankrupted if he had lost. "I feel very sorry for Ian Botham," he added.

Botham said he was "astonished" by the verdict, but had no regrets. "I fought for my dignity and honesty," he said. To cover the bill, he plans to take part in more "Beefy and Lamby" roadshows around the country.

Imran Khan – who said he was "overjoyed" by the verdict – leaving court with his wife Jemima, daughter of Sir James Goldsmith.

ATLANTA, GEORGIA, WED. 31

Injury and illness dog UK athletes

Sally Gunnell leaving the hurdles track.

A disappointing week for British Olympic hopes began on Sunday with runner Liz McColgan's finishing sixteenth in the women's marathon – due, she said, to falling sick after being bitten by an insect. On Monday, an Achilles tendon injury forced Sally Gunnell to pull out of the 400-m hurdles in the semi-finals. And Linford Christie's quest for gold came to an end yesterday when he failed to qualify for the men's 200 m. (→ August 4)

Kew Gardens, Wednesday 31. Crowds gathered to see – and smell – the rare titan arum lily as it bloomed for the first time in 33 years, giving off a distinctive odour of rotting flesh.

GENEVA, TUESDAY 30

Nuclear powers discuss ban while China sets off "last" blast

China conducted what it says will be its last nuclear test yesterday, at the same time as negotiators from 61 countries were meeting in Geneva to complete a global test ban agreement.

China, the last nuclear power to halt testing, said that it would impose a moratorium following Monday's test in the northwestern Xinjiang region. The announcement was welcomed by Western nuclear powers and Russia, who have all agreed to a compromise text of the Comprehensive Test Ban Treaty under discussion in Geneva.

Objections by China and India may delay an agreement, however. China disagrees with proposals for on-site verification, while India is refusing to sign the proposal unless the five main nuclear powers commit to full disarmament. (→ September 10)

Atlanta goes for gold

THE CENTENNIAL Olympic Games came to Atlanta, Georgia, thanks to the tireless efforts of a local property lawyer, Billy Payne. It seemed to many an unlikely location for such a massive event, but there is no doubt, at least in the minds of Georgians, that the city succeeded.

The bomb in the Olympic village, which killed two and injured more than 100, will remain a blot on the memory of the Games. And foreigners grumbled about excessive commercialization, inadequate bus services, and glitches in the IBM results system. But with a US medal tally topping 100, Americans loved the Games.

Outstanding memories

The memories that will linger longest are two outstanding examples of moral and physical courage. First it was Muhammad Ali at the opening ceremony, proving he is still the Greatest by lighting the Olympic flame despite the terrible ravages of Parkinson's disease. Then it was Kerri Strug, the gymnast who leapt the pain barrier to perform with a damaged ankle and won the heart of America.

There was no lack of superlative athletic performances to cheer. Top of the list has to be Michael Johnson, winner of the 400-m and 200-m races, breaking a world record that had stood for 17 years. Black South African Josia Thugwane capped the Games with his win in the men's marathon; and Nigeria became the first African nation to win a world football competition, taking the soccer gold.

Disappointing notes

But for Britain it was a frustrating Olympics. Hero after hero fell by the wayside, and the medal tally was the lowest for 20 years. Rowers Steve Redgrave and Matthew Pinsent provided the country's only gold.

Many observers felt the Olympics had become too big. Some new events were widely ridiculed – beach volleyball, for example, did not strike everyone as a valid Olympic sport.

But even if these Olympics were not rated "the greatest ever", the world had come to Atlanta, Georgia, and fulfilled Billy Payne's dream.

Triumph: Michael Johnson sets a new world record of 19.32 seconds in the 200 m.

Concentration: Lisa Leslie helps the US women's basketball team beat Japan.

Drama: Canada's Donovan Bailey is first across the 100-m finishing line, setting a new world record of 9.84 seconds.

Novelty: The US women's beach volleyball team compete at the new Olympic sport.

Tears: US freestyle wrestler Kurt Angle breaks down after winning gold in the 100 kg.

Heroine: Ireland's Michelle Smith wins a third gold with victory in the 200-m medley.

Courage: Kerri Strug contributes to the US women's gymnastics team victory.

Muscle: Russia's Andrei Chemerkin clinches gold with a 260 kg world-record lift.

The people's Olympics

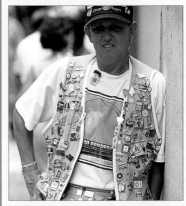

Badge-trading thrived at this most commercial of Games.

A statuesque performance artist draws glances from the crowd.

The purpose-built stadium will serve Atlanta for years to come.

A visitor marks the Centennial Games in idiosyncratic style.

S	M	T	W	T	F	S
				1	2	3
4	5	6	7	8	9	10
11	12	13	14	15	16	17
18	19	20	21	22	23	24
25	26	27	28	29	30	31

Britain, 5
A new hotline is introduced that allows people to denounce their neighbours for benefit fraud.

Atlanta, Georgia, 5
Security guard Richard Jewell, a suspect in the Atlanta bombing, threatens to sue the FBI. (→ October 28)

Washington, DC, 5
President Clinton defies EU allies by signing a bill that would penalize companies – from any country – that invest in oil projects in Iran and Libya.

Rome, 5
Erich Priebke, the former German Nazi SS Captain freed by a court in Rome despite admitting a part in a wartime massacre of Italian civilians, is rearrested at Germany's request.

France, 6
A DNA test clears the tramp, Patrice Padé, who confessed to murdering British schoolgirl Caroline Dickinson.

London, 6
As pro-life groups bring a court injunction to stop the now famous twin abortion, it is revealed that the operation actually took place a month ago. (→ August 15)

Bujumbura, Burundi, 6
Tanzania becomes the first country to enforce the embargo against Burundi by blocking oil at the landlocked country's border. (→ August 20)

London, 7
Outspoken shadow cabinet member Clare Short publicly attacks "new" Labour, and describes leader Tony Blair's advisers as "dark forces".

West London, 8
Sixties fashion designer Ossie Clark is found stabbed to death in his Notting Hill council flat. His flatmate, Diego Cogolato, is charged with the murder.

Deaths
August 2. Michel Debre, former French prime minister, at Montlouis-sur-Loire, aged 84.

August 4. Geoff Hamilton, television gardener, at Merthyr Tydfil, aged 59.

August 9. Sir Frank Whittle, inventor of the jet engine, in Columbia, Maryland, aged 89.

MOSCOW, FRIDAY 9
Yeltsin inauguration prompts fresh health fears

Boris Yeltsin, showing obvious signs of poor health, is sworn in as Russia's president.

A frail-looking Boris Yeltsin was inaugurated today as Russia's first democratically elected leader in the post-Communist era.

The president, who has not been seen in public since June 26, spent only 16 minutes on stage, performing his duties with obvious difficulty. His speech was slurred during the oath of office, and he delivered no inaugural remarks to the 3,000 dignitaries who watched on in silence.

What should have been a historic celebration was further overshadowed by events in Chechenia, where a rebel offensive in Grozny entered its fourth day. More than 120 Russian soldiers are reported dead and 400 wounded in the worst fighting since 1994. (→ September 6)

HERTFORDSHIRE, FRIDAY 9
Commuter train in head-on crash near Watford Junction

A woman has been killed and 69 injured after a commuter train from Euston to Milton Keynes collided with an empty train near Watford Junction yesterday. The crash happened at 5:04 p.m., and rescue crews worked into the night freeing passengers from the wreckage.

Initial reports suggest that the empty train crossed on a line in the path of the oncoming passenger train. The force of the impact sent the two trains into the air, bringing down power lines and leaving carriages strewn across four tracks.

Aerial view of the Watford Junction crash.

BIESCAS, SPAIN, THURSDAY 8
Flash flood devastates Spanish campsite, killing 100 holidaymakers

The Virgen de las Nieves campsite after the flood that left approximately 100 dead.

One hundred people are feared dead and 200 were injured after a river burst its banks and swept through a holiday campsite in the Pyrenees. The disaster struck at about 7 p.m. last night, when the River Gállego, swollen after hours of rain, surged through the popular Virgen de las Nieves campsite near Biescas. Most of the victims were Spanish, although French, German, and Belgian holidaymakers were also among the dead.

By this evening rescue workers had pulled 72 bodies from the mud – some as far as 16 km (10 miles) away from the camp. Prime Minister José Maria Aznar toured the devastated area, declaring it "a ghastly sight".

Meteorite yields clues to life on Mars

Scientists believe a Martian meteorite may hold possible evidence of early life on Mars.

NASA officials announced today that US scientists have found in a Martian meteorite signs that a primitive form of life may have existed on Mars more than three billion years ago.

A NASA statement said that scientists had discovered circumstantial evidence of early life forms in a Martian meteorite that landed on earth 13,000 years ago, and was recovered in Antarctica in 1984. NASA administrator Daniel Goldin stressed, "We are not talking about 'little green men'. These are extremely small single-cell structures."

A scientist familiar with the study said the finding was "unequivocal", and described it as "one of the biggest discoveries ever". (→ October 31)

Atlanta, Georgia, Saturday 3. Muhammad Ali is awarded an honorary gold medal to replace one from the 1960 Olympics in Rome that he threw away after a racist incident in the US.

LONDON, SUNDAY 4

Twin abortion ignites ethics row

Pro-life campaigners have offered £45,000 to a woman who reportedly plans to abort one twin because she cannot afford two more children. Press reports say Professor Phillip Bennett of Queen Charlotte's Hospital is due to perform the selective abortion on a single woman in straitened circumstances who already has one child. The British Medical Association defends the case, but anti-abortion campaigners are calling the operation morally wrong. (→ August 6)

ROME, THURSDAY 1

Ex-Nazi cleared on war crimes charge

Former Nazi SS Captain Erich Priebke was freed today after a military court in Rome ruled he was only following orders when he took part in the massacre of 335 Italian civilians during the Second World War.

Relatives of victims screamed and wept as the verdict was announced, and blocked Priebke from leaving the courtroom for four hours. Shimon Samuels of the Simon Wiesenthal Centre, which helped to hunt down Priebke in Argentina, said bitterly after the verdict: "Italy endorses crimes against humanity". (→ August 5)

Former Nazi SS officer Erich Priebke.

Atlanta, Georgia, Sunday 4. With his victory in the men's marathon, Josia Thugwane becomes the first black South African to win an Olympic gold medal. His countrymen cheered news of his win, and President Mandela dubbed him "South Africa's golden boy".

ATLANTA, GEORGIA, SUN. 4

Poor British show ends in Atlanta

The Atlanta Games came to a close today, ending the worst British performance for 20 years. Britain won 15 medals, only one of which was gold.

The poor state of British sport funding was underscored when two British divers revealed they had to sell their sports kit to pay for a night out. "We haven't got any sponsorship so what are we supposed to do?" said national diving champion and four-time Olympian Robert Morgan.

Breast-beating aside, the Games continued to provide enthralling sports images to the very end: on Friday US sprinter Michael Johnson smashed his own 200-m world record by 0.34 seconds to become the first man ever to win both the 200-m and 400-m races at the same Olympics.

August

S	M	T	W	T	T	S
				1	2	3
4	5	6	7	8	9	10
11	12	13	14	15	16	17
18	19	20	21	22	23	24
25	26	27	28	29	30	31

London, 11
Manchester United resoundingly defeat Newcastle 4–0 in the Charity Shield at Wembley.

New York, 11
Willie King receives a three-year prison sentence for mugging the 94-year-old mother of mafia boss Vincent Gigante. King owned up after discovering the identity of his victim.

Budapest, 11
French-Canadian racing-car driver Jacques Villeneuve wins the Hungarian Grand Prix. (→ September 1)

Liverpool, 12
The Reverend Christopher Gray is stabbed to death outside his church.

Argentina, 12
Diego Maradona announces that he is leaving his football club, Boca Juniors, after missing five consecutive penalties. He is going to a clinic in Switzerland to be treated for cocaine addiction.

Louisville, Kentucky, 12
US golfer Mark Brooks wins the 78th US PGA tournament and $430,000 in prize money.

New York, 14
NASA scientists believe that Europa, a moon of the planet Jupiter, is covered in frozen water, and might contain evidence of life.

London, 15
Princess Diana takes out an injunction against photographer Martin Stenning, banning him from coming within 275 m (300 yd) of her.

London, 15
A women who had one healthy twin embryo terminated on grounds of poverty is found not to be a struggling single parent, as first stated, but a wealthy company director's wife.

Birmingham, 16
Octuplet mother-to-be, Mandy Allwood, is told her health authority will not pay £500,000 for treatment by a London specialist. (→ August 20)

Deaths
August 12, Sir Anthony Parsons, British diplomat, aged 73.

August 13, Marshal Antonio Spinola, soldier and former president of Portugal, aged 86.

MOSCOW, FRIDAY 16
Lebed attacks Moscow leadership

Given sweeping powers by President Yeltsin to end the war in Chechenia, security advisor General Alexander Lebed has demanded the sacking of the newly appointed interior minister, Anatoli Kulikov. A former general, Kulikov was one of the men responsible for sending Russian troops into Chechenia, and Lebed regards him as an inept "Napoleon" bent on death and destruction.

This demand is a typical piece of brinkmanship from the pugnacious Lebed, who believes that Russia cannot afford to continue its costly occupation of Chechenia. The Russian troops continue to suffer at the hands of the rebels, but General Lebed remains confident that he can broker a face-saving peace. (→ August 23)

Peace negotiator Alexander Lebed.

PHILIPPINES, SUNDAY 11
Volcano eruption kills conservationist

A British student was killed yesterday when a volcano exploded without warning. Julian Green, 21, was hit on the head by a rock after the eruption of Mount Canlaon. Two Filipinos, Noel Tragico and Noel Perez, were also killed in the eruption. Mr. Green died in the arms of fellow British adventurer Gordon Cole, who was praised by survivors for his courage in helping them down the mountain.

CHARLEROI, BELGIUM, SATURDAY 17
Girls' bodies found in Belgian house of horror

Marc Dutroux (right) is arrested and led away by Belgian police.

Belgian police dug up the bodies of two girls and an adult today in the garden of a house owned by 39-year-old Marc Dutroux. Yesterday police found two other girls shackled in an underground chamber in the house. Both had been sexually abused.

The dead girls have been identified as Melissa Russo and Julie Lejeune, both aged eight, who had been missing for 14 months. They apparently starved to death while Dutroux was in police custody on another matter.

Dutroux was a known paedophile. Police twice visited his house during

Melissa Russo (left) and Julie Lejeune.

the search for the missing girls, but did not find them. Convicted for paedophile offences in 1989, Dutroux served only three years of a 13-year sentence. (→ August 21)

Northholt, Tuesday 13. A Learjet landing at RAF Northholt overshot the runway and crashed into a van on a dual carriageway. The three people on the plane escaped with only minor injuries, as did the van driver, who said simply, "I am happy to be alive".

DHERINIA, CYPRUS, SUNDAY 11

Cypriot bikers' protest ends in death

Tassos Isaac, a Greek Cypriot, has been beaten to death, and more than 50 Greek and Turkish Cypriots wounded today, in the worst clashes for years between the two communities on the partitioned island.

Hundreds of Greek Cypriot motorcyclists defied a government order to cancel a mass protest against Turkey's continuing occupation of northern Cyprus. Fighting broke out as the bikers attempted to penetrate into the Turkish-held areas. British troops of the UN peace-keeping force were unable to prevent this latest upsurge in violence.

Greek Cypriot bikers drive to the border zone to confront the Turkish Cypriot authorities.

Britain, Monday 12. Church leaders attack the Conservative party's anti-Labour campaign depicting Labour leader Tony Blair with demonic eyes.

LONDON, SUNDAY 11

Mother decides on eight–baby birth

A young woman who is pregnant with eight embryos has sold her story to the *News of the World* – but the deal is raising ethical questions over her decision to keep all the embryos.

Mandy Allwood has been advised to undergo a selective abortion of six embryos or face losing all eight and putting her own life at risk. But the *News of the World* deal partially depends upon Ms. Allwood having all eight children. An unrepentant Ms. Allwood said: "I want nature to take its course ... as far as I am concerned, the more the merrier." (→ August 16)

SEOUL, SOUTH KOREA, THURSDAY 15

Students fight for reunification

Backed by helicopters, South Korean riot police stormed a university in Seoul today for the second day running, to end demonstrations by students calling for reunification with communist North Korea. Students hurled stones and petrol bombs at the police, who replied with volleys of tear gas, which dispersed the students to the shelter of campus buildings. The police had originally decided to enter the university to stop the protesters from marching to the border with North Korea for a joint rally.

SAN DIEGO, CALIFORNIA, THURSDAY 15

Republican nominee Dole stresses trust in US

In his acceptance speech for the Republican party nomination yesterday, Bob Dole made the standard promises to balance the budget and cut taxes. He refused to jump on the right-wing bandwagon, and emphasized the need for "inclusion" and "compassion" in government, which, he said, depended on the trust of the American people.

As in any well-managed television event, dissenting voices were kept in the background, and the controversial issue of abortion – which had threatened to cause acrimony between the pro-life and pro-choice wings of the party – was almost never mentioned by podium speakers.

The success of the convention owed much to the choice of former rival Jack Kemp as vice-presidential running mate, and to the presence of Dole's charismatic wife, Elizabeth, who left the stage to walk among the delegates and talk about the "man I love". (→ November 6)

Bob and Elizabeth Dole wave to a cheering crowd at the Republican party convention in San Diego.

August

S	M	T	W	T	F	S
				1	2	3
4	5	6	7	8	9	10
11	12	13	14	15	16	17
18	19	20	21	22	23	24
25	26	27	28	29	30	31

Washington, DC, 18
Ross Perot becomes Reform party candidate for the presidency, brushing aside a challenge from former Colorado governor Richard Lamm.

Canberra, 19
More than 60 police and demonstrators are hurt in clashes outside Canberra's Parliament House prior to the announcement by Prime Minister John Howard of £2 billion-worth of cuts in the new coalition government's first budget.

Durham, 19
The coroner at the inquest into the death of student Peter Hall from a new strain of CJD, records a verdict of misadventure. He says Hall probably contracted the disease by eating beefburgers contaminated with BSE.

London, 19
Actress Koo Stark, 40, announces that she is pregnant but says she will probably never reveal the name of the father unless he and the child wish it.

The Philippines, 19
President Fidel Ramos and Muslim rebel leader Nur Misuari agree to work out a deal to end the 26-year rebellion in Mindanao.

Seoul, South Korea, 20
Korean riot police clear protestors from Seoul university campus in a dawn raid. The students are demanding that US troops withdraw from Korea and that North and South Korea be reunited.

London, 20
John Major gives a peerage to advertising tycoon Maurice Saatchi, the creator of the Tory "demonic eyes" poster campaign against the Labour party.

Bujumbura, Burundi, 20
Burundi's military leader, Major Pierre Buyoya, dismisses three key military officers in a bid for international approval and an end to trade sanctions.

London, 20
The NHS agrees to pay an estimated £500,000 for multiple-birth specialist, Kypros Nicolaides, to care for Mandy Allwood, who is carrying eight foetuses. (→ October 2)

NEW YORK, SUNDAY 18
Clinton celebrates 50th birthday at star-studded event

Chelsea Clinton helps her father to blow out the 50 birthday candles while Hillary looks on.

New York's Radio City Music Hall was tonight the setting for the most lavish presidential birthday party since Marilyn Monroe serenaded John F. Kennedy in 1962. President Clinton is 50 and had singers from the five decades of his life to entertain him, from Tony Bennett to Shania Twain. Whoopi Goldberg hosted the show, which was broadcast to fundraising venues across the US.

President Clinton needs to regain the initiative after the triumphal Republican convention. This week he signs new health-care legislation and a welfare bill that will end the universal safety-net for the poor created 60 years ago by the New Deal. Although controversial, these measures are likely to increase the president's chances of re-election.

PARIS, SATURDAY 24
French celebrities back immigrants

Riot police stormed the Saint Bernard church in the Goutte d'Or district of Paris yesterday, evicting 300 African immigrants, including ten who had been on hunger strike for 50 days. Even though many have lived in the country for years, the immigrants face expulsion from France under immigration laws that were passed in 1993.

President Chirac issued the order to send in the riot police despite enormous popular support for the immigrants. French celebrities, including actress Emmanuelle Béart, had gathered at the church, hoping to prevent the expulsion, and several thousand protestors marched through Paris last night. (→ August 25)

Riot police fight their way through demonstrators outside Saint Bernard church.

London, Wednesday 21. Crowds flocked to an exact replica of Shakespeare's Globe Theatre that opened tonight on the south bank of the Thames, the spot where the original theatre stood 400 years ago.

SOUTH AFRICA, MONDAY 19
Fresh shooting sparks panic

A German business executive, Erich Ellmer, was shot dead outside his home in Johannesburg yesterday, in an attempted kidnapping that went wrong. The murder highlights the increasing levels of violence and drug-related crime in South Africa.

With the police apparently impotent, ordinary people are increasingly turning to armed vigilantes to counter the crime wave. A Muslim vigilante group publicly murdered a drug dealer in the Cape Flats area of Cape Town last week.

CHARLEROI, BELGIUM, WEDNESDAY 21

Belgian paedophile hunt extends abroad

Belgian police are today seeking help from other forces in Europe to track down the paedophile ring thought to be associated with Marc Dutroux, arrested for the killing of two young girls. At present the police have no firm leads, as they are heavily dependent on Dutroux's confession. He denies killing the girls, Melissa Russo and Julie Lejune, claiming they were murdered by an accomplice whom he subsequently killed in a fit of rage.

The police are also investigating how Dutroux, a 39-year-old electrician of modest means, managed to acquire 11 properties in Belgium. This suggests that he has received money from elsewhere, backing his claim that he abducted children in order to sell them abroad. (→ September 3)

Relations mourn at the coffins of Melissa Russo and Julie Lejune.

NORFOLK, MONDAY 19

Two children go missing on beach

Six-year-old Jodi Loughlin and her four-year-old brother, Tom, went missing yesterday from the beach at Holme next the Sea near Hunstanton in Norfolk. They were last seen running towards the sea at 5:30 p.m.

More than 100 volunteers joined the parents, police, coastguards, and helicopters in scouring the beach, salt marshes, and sand dunes for the children until 1 a.m., without success. The search is due to begin again at first light. (→ August 30)

WESTMINSTER, SATURDAY 24

Early release of prisoners halted by Howard

About 80 prisoners have been freed early after legal advice to the Prison Service suggested their sentences had been wrongly calculated. The confusion concerned how time on remand was deducted from the sentences of those guilty of more than one crime.

The freeing of serious offenders on a technicality has caused a public outcry. Last night Michael Howard, the Home Secretary, suspended further releases pending new legal advice.

GROZNY, CHECHENIA, FRIDAY 23

Russia ends bombardment of Grozny and signs ceasefire

As the ceasefire takes effect, a resident of Grozny walks through the battered remains of the Chechen capital.

After days of ferocious bombardment, Russian guns fell silent in Grozny at 9 a.m. The ceasefire was engineered by national security chief Alexander Lebed yesterday. Under the agreement, Russian troops will pull back from positions near Chechen strongholds. This will leave the Chechen guerrillas in control of most of Grozny, which they captured from the Russian forces after an audacious assault on the city on August 6.

Lebed's concessions to the rebels reflect his belief that Russia cannot win a military victory. His approach is popular with the war-weary Russian people, but he has been criticized by President Yeltsin. (→ August 31)

New York, Wednesday 21. The flamboyant, cross-dressing US basketball star, Dennis Rodman, signs copies of his new book, *Bad as I Wanna Be*, sporting a wedding dress, a blond wig, and bright red lipstick.

S	M	T	W	T	F	S
				1	2	3
4	5	6	7	8	9	10
11	12	13	14	15	16	17
18	19	20	21	22	23	24
25	26	27	28	29	30	31

Paris, 25
The French authorities allow 45 of the 220 illegal immigrants detained at the end of the Saint Bernard church siege last week to stay in the country.

The Oval, 26
Pakistan win the final test against England to take the series 2-0. Pakistan bowler Wasim Akram captures his 300th Test wicket.

Pretoria, 27
Former South African police colonel Eugene de Kock is convicted of six murders committed during the apartheid era. (→ September 18)

Jerusalem, 28
Palestinian leader Yassir Arafat calls for a campaign of civil disobedience against the Israeli authorities, following the demolition of an Arab community centre. (→ September 4)

Faslane, 28
The last British Polaris submarine is decommissioned at Faslane naval base on the Clyde.

Portsmouth, 29
Liam Botham, 19-year-old son of the famous cricketer Ian, makes his first appearance for Hampshire against Middlesex and takes five wickets.

Brentwood, Essex, 30
Former world heavyweight champion Frank Bruno announces his retirement from the boxing ring.

Norfolk, 30
The body of Jodi Loughlin, aged six, is washed up on a beach 50 km (30 miles) east of Holme next the Sea, where she disappeared with her brother 13 days ago. (→ September 1)

Iraq, 31
US troops are put on standby as Iraqi troops seize the town of Arbil in the Kurdish "safe haven" in the north of Iraq. (→ September 3)

South Africa, 31
Nelson Mandela confirms that he is having an affair with Graca Machel, the widow of Mozambique's former leader, Samora Machel.

London, 31
The Labour party announces that it has received a donation of £1 million from an animal welfare group, the Political Animal Lobby.

Lebed signs peace deal with Chechens

Shaking hands for peace: Aslan Maskhadov (left) and Alexander Lebed.

Russian National Security Advisor, Alexander Lebed, signed a peace treaty today with Chechen leader Aslan Maskhadov. After eight hours of talks, Lebed emerged from the meeting with the Chechen rebels to announce: "That is it, the war is over." The treaty, which ends nearly two years of war in which at least 30,000 people have died, is clearly a diplomatic fudge. Russian troops will withdraw from Chechenia, but the status of the country will not be finally decided until after December 31, 2001.

Russian hardliners will claim that the treaty is a sell-out to the Chechens, but Lebed has been prepared to stake his political reputation on the war's unpopularity with the Russian people. (→ September 3)

STANSTED, TUESDAY 27
Iraqis hijack plane and flee to Britain

Seven Iraqi hijackers gave themselves up to security forces at Stansted airport today, following eight hours of negotiation. The aircraft, a Sudan Airways Airbus with 199 people on board, was hijacked on a flight from Khartoum to Jordan yesterday, and diverted to Britain after a refuelling stop in Cyprus.

After their surrender to the British authorities, the hijackers immediately applied for political asylum. It is thought that they are dissidents who had been recalled to Iraq, and, fearful for their safety, decided to seek refuge in the United Kingdom.

Armed police board the aircraft after the surrender of the Iraqi hijackers.

London, Monday 26. An estimated 800,000 people attended this year's Notting Hill Carnival. One man was critically injured after a stabbing in what was otherwise a peaceful and festive occasion.

CHICAGO, THURSDAY 29

Clinton proclaims, "Hope is back"

A riot of flags, balloons and banners welcome President Bill Clinton to the Democratic convention in Chicago.

President Bill Clinton's acceptance speech tonight ended the Democratic National Convention on a high note. The scandal of Clinton aide Dick Morris's resignation was put aside as the party closed ranks behind their president. Pledging to "build a bridge to the 21st century", Clinton told delegates that "hope is back in America".

The four-day build-up to the nomination had been smoothly managed. Hillary and Chelsea Clinton were given prominence to stress the Democratic commitment to family values. Jim Brady, disabled in the Reagan assassination attempt in 1981, made an emotional appearance with his wife to plead for gun controls, and Christopher Reeve made a moving appeal for aid for Americans with disabilities. (→ November 6)

CHICAGO, THURSDAY 29

Clinton aide resigns over call-girl scandal

The man largely credited with engineering Bill Clinton's recent political comeback has resigned today amid reports that he gave administration secrets to a prostitute. Dick Morris was named by the *Star*, a US tabloid, as hiring a $200-an-hour prostitute and allowing her to listen to a phone call from the president. The *Star* also claims Morris gave the prostitute a copy of a Hillary Clinton speech five days before it was delivered.

The White House refused to comment on the allegations, but in a statement President Clinton said, "Dick Morris is my friend and he is a superb political strategist".

Front cover of the Star, *which broke the news of the Dick Morris scandal.*

LONDON, WEDNESDAY 28

Royal marriage ends with a rubber stamp

The 15-year marriage of the Prince and Princess of Wales ended today at Somerset House, with a civil servant's stamp granting a decree absolute. The prime minister, John Major, said that there was no prospect of an early remarriage for Prince Charles, despite the continuation of his long-term relationship with Camilla Parker Bowles.

The Princess of Wales, who is to be stripped of the title Her Royal Highness, began her new life as a single woman by attending a long-standing lunchtime engagement at the English National Ballet in South Kensington. Significantly, perhaps, she continued to wear her wedding and engagement rings.

Manchester, Wednesday 28. Cyclist Chris Boardman broke the world record for the 4,000-m pursuit at the world track cycling championships this evening. He took more than six seconds off the record set by Andrea Collinelli at the Olympic Games in Atlanta.

SEOUL, MONDAY 26

South Korean president faces death sentence

A former South Korean president, Chun Doo Hwan, was today sentenced to death for masterminding a military coup in 1979 and ordering a massacre of civilian demonstrators in the city of Kwangju the following year. His co-defendant and successor as president, Roh Tae Woo, was jailed for 22 years for his role in the coup.

Other South Korean business and military leaders received lesser sentences, as part of current President Kim Young Sam's campaign to "right the wrongs of history". Relatives of those killed in the Kwangju massacre cheered at the news of Chun's death sentence. However, it is thought likely that he could benefit from a presidential pardon.

September

Norfolk, 1
The body of Tom Loughlin, the four-year-old boy who disappeared with his sister two weeks ago from a Norfolk beach, is found washed up on a beach at Sheringham 50 km (30 miles) away.

Somerset, 1
Six young people are killed in a car crash returning from a music festival near Frome. Two of them were grand-children of the First World War poet Siegfried Sassoon.

Lord's, London, 3
Outgoing chairman of the England selectors, Ray Illingworth, is cleared on appeal of bringing the game into disrepute.

New York, 3
British Tennis No. 1 Tim Henman fails to reach the quarter-finals of the US Open, after his defeat by Stefan Edberg in four sets. (→ September 8)

Charleroi, Belgium, 3
In the Belgian paedophile murder case, police find two more bodies buried in the garden of a house owned by Marc Dutroux. They are identified as missing girls An Marchal, 17, and Eefje Lambrecks, 19. (→ October 19)

Moscow, 3
General Lebed says the death toll in the 21-month Chechen conflict may have reached 90,000, with hundreds of thousands injured.

Arabian Gulf, 4
The US launches a second missile strike against Iraq, amid reports of continuing Iraqi shelling in northern Kurdish areas. (→ September 9)

New York, 5
Accused terrorist Ramzi Ahmed Yousef is found guilty of plotting to blow up 12 US-bound airliners. His apparent aim was to make the US reconsider its Middle East policy.

London, 5
Matthew Harding, vice-chairman of Chelsea football club, promises to give the Labour party £1 million. It is the biggest individual donation yet made to the party.

Sydney, 7
British tourist Brian Hagland is beaten to death on Bondi Beach by two men in an apparently random killing.

US launches 27 missiles against Iraq

The US launched a missile strike against Iraq early this morning, in response to Iraqi incursions into Kurdish safe havens in northern Iraq at the weekend. The attack involved two B52 bombers and two guided missile warships in the Gulf, which fired 27 cruise missiles on targets in southern Iraq. Iraqi sources said five people were killed and 19 injured.

In an address from the Oval Office after the attack, President Clinton said that he had extended one of the two Western-imposed no-fly zones in Iraq. He has also blocked a UN plan, due to take effect later this month, that would allow Iraq to sell oil for food.

Iraqi leader Saddam Hussein was defiant after the attack, declaring the allied no-fly zones "null and void", and ordering his forces to shoot down hostile aircraft patrolling the areas. Western intelligence sources say that Iraqi tanks are moving deeper into northern Kurdish areas, despite Iraq's claims that their troops are withdrawing. Last Saturday, the Iraqi military supported the Kurdish Democratic Party in capturing the city of Irbil from a rival Kurdish faction.

Most of America's allies have condemned the strike, with only Britain offering full support. But US Defense Secretary William Perry said emphatically that the US would take further action if necessary. (→ September 4)

A Tomahawk cruise missile is launched from the US destroyer Laboon in the Gulf.

Kurds fleeing from Iraqi and hostile Kurdish forces queue for water at a refugee camp.

Oxfordshire, Sunday 1. Williams Renault announce they will sack Damon Hill (right) at the end of this season. Team owner Frank Williams (left) is said to have found a replacement. (→ September 22)

Rhino horns seized by police

Police in London have made the world's biggest seizure of rhinoceros horns. Detectives raided garages in Kensington after an investigation carried out in association with the RSPCA. They found 105 horns, worth around £2.8 million. Three arrests were made.

White and black rhinoceroses are among the world's most endangered species, but poaching is rife. Ground rhino horn commands high prices in the Far East, where it is valued as an aphrodisiac. The RSPCA said there were only 13,000 rhinos in existence, so the haul represented almost 1 per cent of the total rhino population.

Yeltsin comes clean on heart operation

Only two months after his re-election as Russia's president, Boris Yeltsin yesterday admitted to the Russian people that he needs heart bypass surgery. In a television interview, Yeltsin said he would undergo the operation before the end of the month. Today there is mounting pressure on him to appoint a temporary replacement as fears of a power vacuum grow. (→ September 19)

Plains, Georgia, Sunday 1. Amy Carter, the 28-year-old daughter of former US President Jimmy Carter, married James Wentzel, 27, in a simple ceremony.

Five Nations Championship rescued

With rugby union in turmoil, it looked as if the popular Five Nations Championship might cease to exist. After England negotiated a unilateral television deal with BSkyB last June, the other nations threatened to expel it from the competition.

But today fevered negotiations produced a compromise to save the championship, as Scotland, Wales and Ireland agreed to make their own Sky TV deals. England's Rugby Football Union remains in dispute with its clubs and players, who boycotted the last England training session.

Leaders shake hands across the divide

Netanyahu (left) and Arafat shake hands at the Erez checkpoint in the Gaza Strip.

The new Israeli prime minister Benyamin Netanyahu once declared that he would never meet with Palestinian leader Yassir Arafat because he considered him a terrorist. But today the two men briefly clasped hands across a table in a gesture that might just put the Middle East peace process back on track.

The one-hour summit meeting at Erez on the Gaza border predictably failed to produce any practical moves towards agreement between the two sides. Arafat continues to call for full implementation of accords signed with the previous Israeli government. Netanyahu pointedly refuses to admit that he might be bound by previous agreements. (→ October 2)

Hurricane Fran devastates the Carolinas, leaving 12 dead

Damage along the coast near Wilmington, North Carolina, which was the largest city to feel the full force of the hurricane.

Hurricane Fran ripped through the Carolinas Thursday night and early Friday, leaving 12 dead and causing millions of dollars' worth of damage. Beach towns were submerged, power supplies to nearly one million homes were lost, and severe flooding was reported in low-lying areas.

The hurricane hit shore near Cape Fear, North Carolina, late Thursday with 182 kph (115 mph) winds. Most of the people killed were motorists whose cars were hit by falling trees. On Friday Fran moved to Virginia and was downgraded to a tropical storm. President Clinton has declared North Carolina a major disaster area, opening the way for federal assistance.

S	M	T	W	T	F	S
1	2	3	4	5	6	7
8	9	10	11	12	13	14
15	16	17	18	19	20	21
22	23	24	25	26	27	28
29	30					

New York, 8
Pete Sampras and Steffi Graf win the singles titles at the US Open tennis championships at Flushing Meadow.

Manchester, 8
Wigan beat St. Helens to win the rugby league premiership trophy at Old Trafford.

New York, 10
The UN General Assembly endorses the Comprehensive Test Ban Treaty, a universal ban on nuclear testing. (→ September 24)

London, 11
Conservative MP Sebastian Coe quits as honorary chairman of the National Pistol Association in disgust at its verbal attacks on the parent of a Dunblane victim. (→ October 3)

Burbank, California, 12
Actress Sondra Locke sues former companion Clint Eastwood for over $2 million, claiming that the star has sabotaged her career.

Athens, 12
The sole beneficiary of the late Greek prime minister Andreas Papandreou is his wife Dimitra Liani-Papandreou (Mimi), a former flight attendant.

Manchester, 12
Peter Martin, 56, a former policeman and modelling agency owner, is jailed for 20 years for raping models in his agency. He also supplied young women to millionaire Owen Oyston, who was jailed for rape in May.

Paris, 12
The French magazine *Paris Match* announces that it has signed the Duchess of York as a regular writer.

Kent, 13
Police officially name Kenneth Noye as the chief suspect in the M25 road-rage killing of Stephen Cameron on May 19. (→ November 4)

Washington, DC, 13
The White House refuses to release Bill Clinton's health records, admitting that they contain details that might "compromise his dignity".

Hertfordshire, 14
England and Arsenal footballer Tony Adams confesses to being an alcoholic, but says he is now "well on the road to recovery".

PIAN DEL RE, ITALY, FRIDAY 13

Italian separatist calls for new state of Padania

The Italian separatist leader of the Northern League, Umberto Bossi, today launched a crusade on the banks of the River Po as a prelude to the declaration of independence for the republic of Padania, his name for northern Italy. After symbolically filling a flask with water from the source of the Po at Pian del Re, he instigated a "March to the Sea" which would culminate in Venice with the proclamation of Padanian independence.

After gaining 10.6 per cent of the vote in the last general election, the Northern League has gained support in northern Italy based on dissatisfaction with high taxes, bureaucracy, and perceived southern inefficiency and crime. (→ September 15)

Italian supporters of the Northern League proclaim an "independent" Padania.

LOS ANGELES, SUNDAY 8

British TV successes win US awards

The eponymous hero of Frasier, *Kelsey Grammer, with his on-screen father.*

Actor Ted Danson in Gulliver's Travels.

Tonight saw the fiftieth anniversary of the US television industry's Emmy awards, and British programmes were among the top winners. *Gulliver's Travels*, which was largely produced and financed in Britain, won five Emmys – the same number as the cult psychic-investigation hit, the *X-Files*. After two previous nominations, British actress Helen Mirren took her first Emmy for her role as detective Jane Tennison in *Prime Suspect*.

The most nominated series, *ER*, won only one out of a possible 17 awards, although this was the prestigious best drama award. *Frasier* won four Emmys, including its third successive award for best comedy.

DUKAN, IRAQ, MONDAY 9

Kurds backed by Iraq triumph over rivals

Kurdish forces supported by President Saddam Hussein's Iraqi government today attacked and routed a rival Kurdish faction. Troops of the Kurdish Democratic Party (KDP) stormed towards the Iranian border, throwing back forces of the Patriotic Union of Kurdistan (PUK) in disarray. KDP forces have also captured the PUK stronghold of Sulaymaniyah. Many Kurds have fled their homes, fearful of the Iraqi involvement in the KDP advance. (→ October 14)

Rome, Sunday 8. Naturalized black Italian Denny Mendez has caused uproar by being voted Miss Italy. There are complaints that the former Dominican does not reflect "Italian beauty".

LITTLE ROCK, ARKANSAS, TUESDAY 10

Former Clinton associate won't testify

In one of the stranger twists in the Whitewater affair, Susan McDougal, a former business partner of President Bill Clinton, has gone to jail rather than testify before a grand jury about the president's role in the Whitewater case. She was being asked to say whether Clinton had helped her obtain an illegal loan.

McDougal has surprised observers by her decision. She could have taken the stand and simply stated the truth of President Clinton's account or denied knowledge of proceedings, thus avoiding the contempt charges.

Yesterday, McDougal was taken to a county jail in Conway, Arkansas, with cuffed hands and manacled feet, facing the possibility of an 18-month sentence for contempt of court. There are already suggestions, however, that she may benefit from a presidential pardon after the November election.

McDougal claims in her defence that the Whitewater special prosecutor, Republican Kenneth Starr, is guilty of partisanship. However, this allegation is not thought to carry much legal weight.

Susan McDougal is handcuffed and led away from court to begin her sentence for contempt.

Venice, Sunday 8. Liam Neeson wins the best actor award at the Venice Film Festival for his performance in the lead role of *Michael Collins*, **which also won the best film award.**

CANTERBURY, TUESDAY 10

Survivor gives murder-hunt police fresh leads

Survivor Josephine Russell is helping police to find the killer of her mother and sister.

Two months ago, nine-year-old Josephine Russell suffered serious head injuries in a frenzied hammer attack outside the Kent village of Chillenden that left both her mother and sister dead. She now has the speech level of a two-year-old.

But with the help of specially trained police officers, Josephine has been able to give a description of a man who may be the assailant. A composite picture of the man has been issued by the police and a hammer found near the scene of the crime is being analyzed to see whether it is the murder weapon.

ZURICH, SATURDAY 14

Stolen Jewish gold held by Swiss banks

Stung by the revelation that Swiss financial institutions have held on to gold stolen from Jews and deposited in bank vaults by the Nazis, the Swiss government will publish a decree next Monday that orders all bank records to be handed over to a special investigating committee.

How much gold is actually in the vaults is disputed, but Jewish groups say that as much as £4 billion at today's prices is still unaccounted for. Swiss sources say that there is only £20 million in the dormant accounts, but, whatever the final figure, the problem remains of finding the rightful owners. At present 700 people are making claims for the money, but one of the lawyers representing the claimants believes that much of the money has been spirited out of the accounts since 1945. (→ October 22)

RIO DE JANEIRO, THURSDAY 12

Amazon rain forest continues to shrink

Despite claims by the Brazilian government that strict environmental laws have slowed the destruction of the Amazonian rain forests, recent figures suggest that forest clearing is on the increase. Deforestation rose by 34 per cent during 1990 to 1994. Brazil has announced measures to crack down on illegal logging but environmentalists argue that this is merely window-dressing to counter hostile world opinion.

Vanishing asset: Brazilian loggers cut a swathe through the Amazonian forest.

September

S	M	T	W	T	F	S
1	2	3	4	5	6	7
8	9	10	11	12	13	14
15	16	17	18	19	20	21
22	23	24	25	26	27	28
29	30					

Venice, 15
Separatist leader Umberto Bossi declares northern Italy independent as "Padania". The declaration has no practical effect.

Monaco, 16
Princess Stephanie of Monaco files for divorce from her husband, Daniel Ducret, following the publication of pictures of him with a stripper.

Santa Monica, California, 17
The civil suit against O. J. Simpson, brought by the parents of Nicole Brown Simpson and Ron Goldman, opens. O. J. will be forced to testify during the trial. (→ October 23)

London, 19
Kevin Maxwell, son of the disgraced media tycoon Robert Maxwell, walks free on fraud charges as a judge calls a second trial "unfair".

Tours, 19
The Pope begins a four-day visit to France, his last foreign trip before he undergoes surgery for an inflamed appendix next month. (→ October 8)

South Korea, 19
South Korean troops shoot seven North Koreans on the second day of a manhunt for infiltrators who came ashore from a submarine. Six more infiltrators are thought to be at large.

Karachi, 20
Murtaza Bhutto, brother and rival of Pakistan's prime minister, Benazir Bhutto, is shot dead by police. The police allege that Murtaza's supporters started a gun battle. (→ October 27)

Moscow, 20
President Boris Yeltsin's doctors publicly express concern about the president's ability to withstand major heart surgery. (→ November 5)

Deaths
September 16. Politician McGeorge Bundy, a key former advisor to Presidents Kennedy and Johnson, in Boston, aged 77.

September 17. Spiro Agnew, former US vice-president under Richard Nixon, in Maryland, aged 77.

September 20. Hungarian Paul Erdos, one of the century's greatest mathematicians, in Warsaw, aged 83.

London, Sunday 15. The former Argentinian World Cup football star, Diego Maradona, demonstrates his ball-control skills to schoolboys who were attending the Puma Street Soccer world finals held in Battersea Park, south London, today.

Yeltsin will hand over control to PM

President Boris Yeltsin last night signed a decree that will hand over all power to the Prime Minister, Viktor Chernomyrdin, while Yeltsin undergoes heart surgery. The move ends a week of debate over who will control the nuclear button while the president is being operated upon.

The issue of who will substitute for Yeltsin has become pressing because of suspicions that he is more ill than officials will admit. He has been out of public life and under medical care almost constantly since his re-election in July. A date is still to be set for his operation. (→ September 20)

AUSTRALIA, SATURDAY 21
Ancient art find confounds theories

Researchers are claiming to have found rock carvings 76,000 years old and 176,000-year-old stone tools in Australia. If correctly dated, the finds undermine current theories about primitive man. Modern *Homo sapiens* was not thought to have reached Australia until 60,000 years ago. This suggests the art and tools were the work of a predecessor, *Homo erectus*, previously thought too unintelligent to have navigated to the antipodes.

Texas, Tuesday 17. Ten thousand new US citizens are sworn in at a mass naturalization ceremony at Texas Stadium, Irving, Texas.

SCOTLAND, FRIDAY 20
Runaway bishop revealed to have a 15-year-old son

Fifteen-year-old Kevin Whibley: "I feel angry at the loss of a father."

The Catholic Church is reeling from scandalous revelations about the private life of the Bishop of Argyll and the Isles, Roderick Wright. Two weeks ago, the 48-year-old bishop disappeared with a divorcee, Mrs. Kathleen Macphee. His resignation from the bishopric was made public last Monday. Today, to the further embarrassment of church leaders, it was revealed that he has a 15-year-old son from an earlier relationship.

Joanna Whibley, age 48, approached BBC TV to reveal her past with the bishop. She told the BBC that her relationship with him developed when the then curate priest counselled her after the breakdown of her marriage. She became pregnant with their son, Kevin Whibley, nearly 16 years ago, but Bishop Wright refused to acknowledge being the father.

Ms. Whibley said she and her son had kept her former lover's secret during his rise up the Church hierarchy, and he had sent them sporadic letters and cheques. Following the news of his resignation, however, she wanted to unburden herself, for her son's sake as well as her own. "I have lived a lie and so has he," she said. A spokesman for the Catholic Church in Scotland said: "Clearly the news does an enormous amount of damage...to the credibility of the Church."

The Bishop of Argyll and the Isles case has provoked a probing debate about the compulsory celibacy of the Catholic priesthood. Cardinal Basil Hume, the leader of the Catholic Church in England and Wales, suggested on Tuesday that the celibacy rule could be changed. "We are losing excellent and very good people because they would wish to be married priests," he said. (→ October 9)

BOSNIA, WEDNESDAY 18

Hardliners hold sway in Bosnia elections

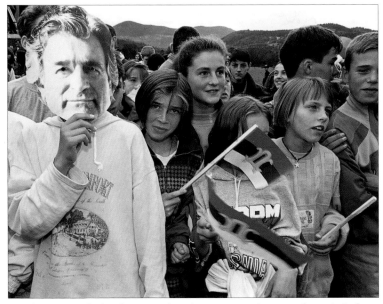

A Serb wears a mask of Radovan Karadzic, showing support for a wanted war criminal.

Muslim supporters of Alija Izetbegovic attend an election rally at Tuzla.

The good news from Bosnia is that elections have taken place without violence. The bad news is that the voters in all three of Bosnia's ethnic groups have backed hardliners who are likely to reinforce the divisions that threaten to tear Bosnia apart.

Under the terms of the Dayton accords that ended the Bosnian civil war last year, Bosnia is to be run by a tripartite presidency, with one representative elected by each ethnic group. The Muslims have elected Alija Izetbegovic, the man who led

them through the civil war. He will chair the presidency. Bosnian Serbs voted for Momcilo Krajisnik, a committed separatist who is under investigation by the War Crimes Tribunal for his part in ethnic cleansing during the civil war. Croats elected Kresimir Zubak, who is said to favour Croatia taking over Croat areas of Bosnia.

It is difficult to imagine these three men working together for peace and harmony. However, US diplomat Richard Holbrooke, the architect of the Dayton accords, said he is just eager to see the new presidential institutions functioning.

SOUTH KOREA, WED. 18

Submarine off coast raises alarm

South Korean troops are hunting for infiltrators from North Korea, after an abandoned submarine was found off South Korea's east coast, near the town of Kangung. The bodies of 11 infiltrators were found in nearby mountains. They had apparently shot themselves to avoid being captured. One soldier was caught alive and has reportedly told his interrogators that 13 other North Korean soldiers are still at large.

Infiltrations are of serious concern to South Korea. Military analysts have warned that a Northern invasion would be preceded by the arrival of saboteurs. (→ September 19)

The abandoned North Korean submarine.

SOUTH AFRICA, WEDNESDAY 18

De Klerk accused by hitman

A former police colonel convicted of being an assassin during the apartheid era has said that F. W. de Klerk, leader of the opposition party in South Africa, knew of covert operations that existed while he was president.

Eugene de Kock headed a secret death squad in the 1980s and early 1990s, and was last month convicted of six murders. During his plea for leniency today, he told the court that de Klerk ordered an attack on a home in Transkei in 1993, where five people were killed. De Klerk has denied knowledge of any atrocities before the Truth and Reconciliation Commission. (→ September 26)

BASINGSTOKE, FRIDAY 20

Jockey Carson in intensive care

Willie Carson on his way to hospital.

Willie Carson, five times champion jockey, is in intensive care tonight at the North Hampshire Hospital in Basingstoke after being kicked in the stomach by a horse. He has severe lacerations to the liver. The incident happened at Newbury race course,

At the age of 53, Willie Carson was already thought to be racing in his last season. He rode his first winner 33 years ago at Catterick.

Washington, DC, Sunday 15. Bill Clinton awards the Presidential Medal of Freedom to 83-year-old Rosa Parks, the woman who sparked the modern civil rights movement 41 years ago when she refused to give up her bus seat to a white passenger in Alabama.

September

S	M	T	W	T	F	S
1	2	3	4	5	6	7
8	9	10	11	12	13	14
15	16	17	18	19	20	21
22	23	24	25	26	27	28
29	30					

Estoril, Portugal, 22
Jacques Villeneuve defeats Damon Hill in the Portuguese Grand Prix. The drivers' world championship now hangs on the last race of the season, the Japanese Grand Prix. (→ September 27)

London, 23
Author Colin Dexter reveals the first name of his famous creation, Inspector Morse. The name is Endeavour.

New York, 24
The five acknowledged nuclear powers – the United States, Britain, France, Russia and China – sign the Comprehensive Test Ban Treaty at the United Nations. The treaty bans all testing of nuclear devices.

London, 26
Former singer Bob Geldof applies for custody of his three children after the police allegedly find drugs at the home of the children's mother, television presenter Paula Yates.

Johannesburg, 26
Eugene de Kock, head of a South African police hit squad during the apartheid era, claims a South African intelligence agent killed the Swedish prime minister Olaf Palme in 1986.

London, 27
Driver Damon Hill, dropped by Williams, chooses TWR Arrows as his team for next season. (→ October 13)

Westminster, 30
Conservative MP Neil Hamilton drops a £10-million libel action against the *Guardian* as it is about to go to court. The newspaper accused Hamilton of accepting money in return for asking questions in Parliament. (→ October 5)

Hobart, Tasmania, 30
Martin Bryant pleads not guilty to the Port Arthur massacre in April in which 35 people died. (→ November 21)

London, 30
The Duchess of York considers legal action to prevent publication of recordings of conversations between her and a clairvoyant, Vasso Kortesis.

London, 30
The Nationwide Building Society says house prices have risen by 7 per cent during the last year.

ASCOT, SATURDAY 28
Bookies weep as Dettori wins seven

Flamboyant 25-year-old Sardinian-born Frankie Dettori made racing history at Ascot today, when he became the first jockey ever to ride seven winners on the same day.

After winning the seventh race, on Fujiyama Crest, Dettori was cheered all the way to the winners' enclosure. He told reporters: "I always thought that perhaps one day in my life I might do it at a small meeting, but to do it on such a competitive card is just beyond me. God was on my side."

Bookmakers are thought to have lost around £10 million. The return for an accumulator bet on Dettori's seven mounts was 25,092.5-1

Washington, DC, Tuesday 24. Diana, Princess of Wales, breakfasts with Hillary Clinton at the White House during a visit to the US capital. In the evening, the Princess chaired a celebrity dinner and fashion sale that raised millions of dollars for breast cancer research.

LONDON, TUESDAY 24
IRA man shot dead in police raid

Blood stains the path outside the house where IRA man Diarmuid O'Neill was shot.

The police and MI5 are claiming a major victory over IRA terrorism after a series of raids yesterday at sites in and around London.

The police raids left one suspected terrorist dead and five more under arrest. They also uncovered the largest cache of arms and explosives ever seized in mainland Britain.

The dead man, named as Diarmuid O'Neill, was shot when police raided a guesthouse in Hammersmith. He appears to have been unarmed. The arms cache, found at a warehouse in north London, included ten tons of homemade explosive. Police believe they have foiled a major IRA bombing offensive in Britain. (→ October 7)

DARWIN, WEDNESDAY 25
Patient exercises "right to die"

A terminally ill cancer patient in Australia's Northern Territory has become the first man to end his own life legally under the Territory's 1995 voluntary euthanasia legislation. The patient, who has not been named, used a computer program called Deliverance to activate a lethal injection. The euthanasia law is currently being challenged in Australia's High Court and the Federal parliament.

Bath, Saturday 28. Comedian Leslie Crowther died today, aged 63. He began his TV career on the children's show *Crackerjack* in 1960. More recently, he hosted the game show *The Price Is Right*.

JERUSALEM, FRIDAY 27

Seventy die in clashes as Palestinian anger erupts

Israeli security forces walk past the Dome of the Rock, one of the Muslim holy places at the heart of the current conflict in Jerusalem.

A wounded Palestinian is carried to safety.

A dispute that focuses on the Muslim holy places in Jerusalem has precipitated the worst clashes between Israel and the Palestinians since the peace process began in 1993. Three days of clashes in Jerusalem and towns on the West Bank have left around 70 dead.

The Palestinians rioted in protest at Israel's decision to open a new entrance to a tunnel near Al-Aqsa mosque and the Dome of the Rock in Jerusalem's Old City.

Palestinian security forces fought with Israeli soldiers after the Israelis entered Palestinian-controlled areas in pursuit of rioters. Israel is threatening to send tanks into the West Bank to quell the uprising. (→ October 2)

KABUL, AFGHANISTAN, FRIDAY 27

Taleban Islamic fighters seize control of Kabul

A Taleban guerilla presents a smiling face after the Muslim fighters' takeover of Kabul.

In a dramatic turn to Afghanistan's seemingly endless civil war, forces of the Islamic fundamentalist Taleban group today took control of the Afghan capital, Kabul.

Afghanistan has witnessed chaotic fighting between rival mujahedin guerrilla groups ever since the communist president, Muhammad Najibullah, was deposed in 1992. One of the Taleban's first acts on entering Kabul was to seize Najibullah from a UN compound, and shoot him dead. Najibullah's body was then hanged outside the presidential palace alongside that of his brother. The Taleban leaders have now declared Afghanistan a "completely Islamic country".

Gulbuddin Hekmatyar, the Afghan prime minister, and his defence chief, Ahmed Shah Massoud, have fled from Kabul. Massoud is expected to continue the fight from his power base north of the city. (→ October 4)

Lexington, North Carolina, Wednesday 25. Six-year-old Johnathan Prevette (seen here, bottom left, with his family) has been punished by his school for kissing a classmate. The kiss on the cheek was defined by the school as sexual harassment.

S	M	T	W	T	F	S
		1	2	3	4	5
6	7	8	9	10	11	12
13	14	15	16	17	18	19
20	21	22	23	24	25	26
27	28	29	30	31		

Braintree, Essex, 1
Sarah Cook, the 13-year-old Essex girl whose illegal marriage to a Turkish waiter in January caused a scandal, gives birth to a baby boy.

Lima, Peru, 2
A Peruvian airliner crashes into the Pacific half an hour after taking off from Lima. All 70 people on board are feared dead.

London, 2
Eurotunnel works out a £4-billion rescue package with its financial backers to avert the threat of insolvency.

London, 2
The FTSE stock market index reaches an all-time record high of 4,015 points.

Washington, DC, 2
The Pentagon announces that 5,000 US troops are to start moving into Bosnia to cover the withdrawal of the NATO-led peace force in December.

Blackpool, 3
At the Labour Party conference, Ann Pearston, a mother from Dunblane, makes an emotional appeal for a ban on all handguns. (→ October 16)

Dover, 3
Two shipping companies, P&O and Stena, merge their cross-Channel ferry operations to compete with the Shuttle rail link through the Channel tunnel.

Moscow, 4
Russian president Boris Yeltsin dismisses six senior generals, including General Yevgeni Podkolzin, commander of the paratroops. (→ October 16)

Nairobi, 4
Pakistani batsman Shahid Afridi, said to be 16 years old, scores a century against Sri Lanka off 37 balls, the fastest-ever century in a one-day cricket international.

Sydney, 4
The Super League defeats the Australian Rugby League in a dispute over the future of rugby league in Australia. The decision opens the way for the growth of the sport on a worldwide scale.

Deaths
October 2. Robert Bourassa, former prime minister of Quebec, aged 63.

Middle East summit fails to heal the fresh wounds

The White House summit: From left to right, Arafat, Hussein, Clinton, and Netanyahu.

President Bill Clinton's latest attempt at the role of international peacemaker ended in partial failure today when a hastily organized Middle East peace summit ended without agreement on crucial issues.

The emergency talks, held over two days at the White House, brought the Palestinian leader Yassir Arafat and Israeli prime minister, Benyamin Netanyahu, face to face for the first time since last week's violence in Jerusalem and the West Bank plunged Israel into crisis. President Clinton chaired the meeting. King Hussein of Jordan was also present.

The Israelis and Palestinians agreed to resume talks on the withdrawal of Israeli troops from the West Bank city of Hebron, but were unable to reach agreement on the issues behind the recent violence. (→ October 23)

Nerve gas hit 15,000 US troops

A Pentagon spokesman has admitted today that more than 15,000 US soldiers may have been exposed to nerve or mustard gas during the Gulf War in 1991. The Pentagon first said last year that some Americans might have suffered exposure to chemical weapons, but only 1,100 men were then said to be involved.

The risk of chemical exposure is said to have occurred when US troops blew up Iraqi arms dumps at Khamisiya in southern Iraq.

London, Wednesday 2. Mandy Allwood, the woman who conceived octuplets after taking fertility drugs, lost the last five of her eight foetuses at King's College hospital tonight.

Volcano threatens Iceland

Gas and ash spew out from the volcano underneath Europe's largest glacier.

A volcano is in eruption underneath the largest ice sheet in Europe. It threatens to cause severe floods that could devastate large areas of Iceland.

Bardhabunga volcano is 200 km (130 miles) east of the Icelandic capital, Reykjavik. It lies beneath the Vatnajokull glacier, which covers almost a tenth of the surface of Iceland. Black clouds of ash and gas are spewing out through a fissure in the ice sheet. Experts fear that much of the glacier will melt, raising water levels to catastrophic heights. (→ November 5)

WESTMINSTER, SATURDAY 5

Sleaze accusations damage reputation of parliament

Conservative MP Neil Hamilton was in trouble over cash-for-questions allegations.

The scandal over cash for questions, involving Conservative MP and former trade minister, Neil Hamilton, this week threatened to stain the reputation of parliament as a whole.

Hamilton has admitted accepting gifts and payment in kind worth £10,000 from lobbyist Ian Greer. It is now thought that at least 20 other MPs, mostly Tories, also received paments from the lobbyist. The *Guardian* newspaper has alleged that Neil Hamilton was paid by Harrods owner Mohamed Al Fayed to ask parliamentary questions. (→ October 14)

Blackpool, Tuesday 1. Labour leader Tony Blair delivered an inspirational speech to delegates at his party's annual conference today. He called on voters to give him 1,000 days in government to prepare Britain for the new millennium.

WASHINGTON, DC, FRI. 4

Many mammals face extinction

More than 1,000 mammal species are at risk of extinction, including one third of all primates, humankind's closest animal relatives.

These figures are from the latest Red List of endangered species issued by the IUCN-World Conservation Union. The organization has been monitoring animal survival for 35 years. It now believes that previous Red Lists may have understated the risk to many species.

The major threat to most species is the destruction or pollution of their natural habitats. US interior secretary Bruce Babbitt said the report clearly shows that "unless people of all nations make extraordinary efforts, we face a looming natural catastrophe of almost biblical proportions".

Stockholm, Thursday 3. Polish poet Wislawa Szymborska has been awarded the 1996 Nobel Prize for Literature. The citation praised Szymborska, aged 73, for her "ironic precision". Poland's former president, Lech Walesa, described her as "great of heart and pen".

KABUL, AFGHANISTAN, FRIDAY 4

Taleban drives women under cover

Only very young women, classified as children, are allowed to show their faces in Taleban-ruled Kabul.

After last week's takeover by Taleban guerrillas, the people of Kabul are enjoying a rare interlude of peace. But they are also having to adapt to a rigorous Islamic regime that intends to control every detail of daily life. All government employees have been ordered to grow beards. Television has been banned and music cassettes are being confiscated.

All women except the very young have been ordered to wear a full veil in public. Women have reportedly been beaten with sticks by Taleban fighters for minor infringements of the new dress code, such as showing a few inches of ankle. Women have also been banned from working, a potentially fatal regulation for the many widows who have no other source of income or support. (→ October 10)

S	M	T	W	T	F	S
		1	2	3	4	5
6	7	8	9	10	11	12
13	14	15	16	17	18	19
20	21	22	23	24	25	26
27	28	29	30	31		

Bordeaux, 6
A bomb destroys the Bordeaux office of French prime minister Alain Juppé.

Oakland, Michigan, 7
The so-called "Jenny Jones murder trial" opens. Jonathan Schmitz is accused of shooting Scott Amedure, a gay man who revealed on the Jenny Jones television chat show that he had a crush on Schmitz.

Gloucester, 7
Demolition work begins on 25 Cromwell Street, the site of the Fred and Rosemary West murders.

Rome, 8
The Pope has his appendix removed in a 50-minute operation. Doctors say there are no complications.

Kendal, 9
The former bishop Roderick Wright and his lover Kathleen Macphee emerge from hiding to apologize for the "sadness and pain" caused after they ran away together.

Estonia, 9
Scotland's world cup qualifying match against Estonia is a one-sided affair, as the opposition fails to turn up. England beats Poland 2-1 in their world cup qualifier at Wembley.

Belfast, 9
James Bradwell, the 43-year-old soldier who was seriously injured in the IRA Thiepval bombing on Monday, dies in hospital.

Bournemouth, 10
Tory MP Sir Nicholas Scott, 63, is found face down in the street during the Conservative party conference.

New York, 11
Researchers from the City University of New York claim that women who have undergone an abortion have a 30 per cent higher risk of contracting breast cancer.

New York, 12
Some senior federal air-safety officials say that the most probable cause of the TWA 800 airliner crash in July is mechanical failure.

Deaths
October 12. René Lacoste, French tennis star and sportswear entrepreneur, aged 92.

BOURNEMOUTH, FRIDAY 11

Major stirs Tory faithful

In a well-received final speech at the Conservative Party's annual conference today, Prime Minister John Major presented himself as a man of the people, contrasting his lowly background with the privileged origins of Labour leader Tony Blair.

Declaring his determination to win the next election, Major told delegates: "I did not come from two rooms in Brixton to 10 Downing Street not to go out and fight with every fibre of my being for the things I believe in and the country I love."

The prime minister's speech ended a generally satisfactory conference for the Tories, in which party unity triumphed over divisions on Europe and the economy. Even Chancellor of the Exchequer Kenneth Clarke, who was widely expected to be given a frosty reception by Tory right-wingers, was heartily cheered for a speech promising only "affordable" tax cuts before the election.

HARTFORD, CONNECTICUT, SUNDAY 6

First TV debate leaves polls unchanged

Sticking to issues: The first Clinton-Dole duel is devoid of dramatic flourishes or gaffes.

Republican presidential challenger Bob Dole, trailing in the opinion polls, is looking to his televised debates with President Clinton to swing the public mood in his favour.

But the first debate, broadcast from the Bushnell Auditorium in Hartford, Connecticut, this evening, suggested he would fail to make a dramatic impact. About 70 million Americans tuned in, the largest sign of public interest so far in a campaign that has been dismissed by many as lacklustre. Few are likely to have changed their minds as the two candidates worked over familiar themes from their campaigns in a civilized way, avoiding personal attacks. (→ November 6)

Washington, DC, Saturday 12. An AIDS Memorial Quilt was laid along Washington's Mall this weekend in memory of those killed by the disease. Each square of the 1600 m- (1 mile-) long quilt represents one of 350,000 AIDS victims in the US. Actress Elizabeth Taylor later led a candlelight remembrance march.

Acquittal for apartheid general

General Malan (left) after the verdict.

Many black South Africans were shocked as General Magnus Malan, a former defence minister of the apartheid era, walked free from court today. In what was seen as one of South Africa's trials of the century, Malan and nine others had been accused of authorizing death squads, including one that massacred 13 people in a township in 1987.

Courtroom onlookers cheered the ruling that brought the six-month trial to an end, and a relieved looking Malan said outside the court, "today the truth has prevailed".

Nelson Mandela, the South African president, refused to condemn the not-guilty verdicts. He said: "The judicial findings must be respected, even, or especially, by those who are aggrieved by the result."

Longchamp, Sunday 6. Helissio, a French-trained, three-year-old colt, outruns Europe's finest to win France's *Prix de l'Arc de Triomphe* race. His closest rival, the English horse Pilsudski, finished five lengths behind.

Terrorists bomb army base

Two car bombs exploded inside the Northern Ireland headquarters of the British Army today, injuring more than 30 people. At least one victim is not expected to survive.

Thiepval Barracks in Lisburn is probably the most heavily defended place in Northern Ireland. Somehow the terrorists were able to penetrate the tight security with two explosive-laden vehicles. The first went off in a car park just inside the entrance to the base. The second detonated near the base's medical centre ten minutes later. It was presumably intended to hit casualties being carried for treatment after the first explosion.

No organization has yet said that it carried out the terrorist attack. It is thought to be the work of the IRA or of a breakaway Republican group. Prime minister John Major has described the bombings as "wicked beyond belief". (→ October 9)

New military alliance drives back Taleban fighters

Taleban fighters prepare to resist the counter-attack on Kabul from the north.

When the Taleban occupied Kabul, Afghanistan, last month, it seemed a turning point in the country's relentless warfare. But the Taleban have only succeeded in uniting their foes.

In the small town of Khinjan, 160 km (100 miles) north of Kabul, faction leaders Ahmed Shah Massoud, Abdul Rashid Dustam, and Abdul Karim Kalilli today forged a formidable alliance. Between them, they already control one third of Afghanistan. Now their forces are driving the Taleban back towards Kabul. Still, no force is strong enough to win a victory and impose peace. (→ October 27)

London, Wednesday 9. The *Sun* newspaper admits it was tricked into publishing pictures from a hoax sex-romp video of Princess Diana and James Hewitt yesterday.

Nobel Prize for Timor campaigners

Controversial winner: Jose Ramos-Horta.

The Nobel Peace Prize was awarded today to two campaigners for the independence of East Timor, a former Portuguese colony that has been ruled by Indonesia since 1976.

One of the laureates, Jose Ramos-Horta, is leader of Fretilin, the East Timorese resistance movement. The other is Carlos Belli, the Bishop of the East Timorese capital, Dili. The award praises the two men for their "self-sacrificing contributions for a small but oppressed people".

The Indonesian government has expressed annoyance over the choice of Mr. Ramos-Horta as a Peace Prize recipient, describing him as "a political adventurist". (→ October 15)

October

S	M	T	W	T	F	S
		1	2	3	4	5
6	7	8	9	10	11	12
13	14	15	16	17	18	19
20	21	22	23	24	25	26
27	28	29	30	31		

Iraq, 14
Kurdish forces hostile to President Saddam Hussein's Iraqi government recover most of the ground lost in last month's fighting in northern Iraq.

Westminster, 14
Speaker of the House of Commons, Betty Boothroyd, warns that the cash-for-questions allegations are bringing the House into disrepute. Parliament's ombudsman, Sir Gordon Downey, is asked to investigate the allegations. (→ November 11)

East Timor, 15
Indonesian president Suharto visits East Timor but makes it clear he will make no concessions in the wake of the Nobel Peace Prize awards to two East Timor activists.

London, 16
Labour front bencher Claire Short is reunited with the son she gave up for adoption in 1965 – Toby Graham, now a 31-year-old City lawyer.

London, 17
Sixteen-year-old Learco Chindamo of north London is found guilty of killing headmaster Philip Lawrence last December. The judge orders that Chindamo be detained indefinitely. (→ October 21)

Guatemala City, 17
At least 78 people are crushed to death at a World Cup qualifying match between Guatemala and Costa Rica.

Perthshire, 17
Footballer Paul Gascoigne is in trouble after reports that he has battered his wife of 14 weeks, 31-year-old Sheryl Gascoigne. (→ November 1)

New York, 18
Scientists announce they have found an "absolute" link between smoking and lung cancer, proving what statistical studies have long suggested.

Brighton, 19
Nearly 5,000 people attend the first conference of Sir James Goldsmith's Referendum party.

Deaths
13 October. Beryl Reid, actress noted for her performances in *The Killing of Sister George* and *Entertaining Mr. Sloane*, aged 76.

WESTMINSTER, WEDNESDAY 16

Partial gun ban proposed after Dunblane report

In the wake of the report of the Cullen inquiry into the Dunblane massacre, which was published today, the government has announced that it will introduce a ban on all handguns over .22 calibre. Even these will have to be kept at gun clubs.

The government announcement did not satisfy Dunblane parents, however, who are continuing to campaign for a total handgun ban. In a joint statement, they described the government proposals as "a compromise on an issue on which there must be no compromise". Their stand is supported by the Labour party and a small number of Conservative MPs, including David Mellor.

The shooting lobby predictably described the proposals as far too strict. About 160,000 guns will have to be surrendered, with compensation set at an average of £150 per weapon. Gun clubs will be required to increase their security and the issue of firearms licences will be more tightly controlled.

The government has accepted the Cullen report's recommendations for tighter school security and the national monitoring of people who work with children. (→ November 18)

London, Tuesday 15. Rolling Stone Mick Jagger and his wife, model Jerry Hall, are reported to be splitting up. Hall is said to have consulted royal divorce lawyer Anthony Julius after press stories appeared linking Jagger with a Czech model.

SUZUKA, JAPAN, SUNDAY 13

Hill clinches world championship with win in Japan

A victorious Hill receives the traditional champagne soaking from drivers Michael Schumacher (left) and Mika Hakkinen (right).

Damon Hill fulfilled his dream of capturing the Formula One world championship yesterday, and he did it in style – winning Japan's Grand Prix, when a sixth place finish would have been enough to secure the title.

Jacques Villeneuve, the only man who could have denied Hill the prize, retired early after losing a rear tyre.

Although Hill had chances at the title earlier in the season, in the end it all hung on the final race. With this triumph, he follows in the footsteps of his late father, Graham Hill, who won two championships in the 1960s. And he proves to Williams Renault, the team that sacked him six weeks ago, that he is without doubt a winner.

Popular protests mount over Belgian paedophile scandal

The Marc Dutroux case, involving the abduction, sexual abuse, and murder of an unknown number of young girls, this week swelled into a massive crisis of confidence in the Belgian political and legal system.

Public outrage peaked on Monday when Jean-Marc Connerotte, the magistrate who first uncovered the paedophile ring, was taken off the case for accepting a meal from campaigners against child abuse. This was said to compromise his impartiality.

Connerotte's removal from the case led to a wave of protests, including strikes by transport workers. Many Belgians fear a cover-up by senior politicians somehow linked to the scandal. A mass demonstration is to be held in Brussels on Sunday.

Belgians mourn lost children and protest against the mishandling of the investigation.

Worcester, Wednesday 16. Lorry driver Stuart Morgan, 37, is found guilty of murdering 19-year-old French student Celine Figard in December last year. Morgan receives the harshest penalty – life imprisonment.

Widow loses battle for baby

A young widow today lost her fight in the High Court for the right to be artificially inseminated with her dead husband's sperm. The judge upheld a ban that prevents 30-year-old Diane Blood from using sperm taken from her dying husband as he lay in a coma. The law requires that sperm donors give written consent. (→ October 20)

Los Angeles, Tuesday 15. Pop star Madonna, seen here in her latest movie role as Evita, gave birth yesterday to a girl, named Lourdes Maria Ciccione Leon. The baby's father is Cuban-born fitness instructor, Carlos Leon.

Yeltsin fires Lebed in dramatic television coup

Russia's most popular politician: General Alexander Lebed, with his wife Inna.

The Russian president, Boris Yeltsin, tonight publicly fired his security chief, General Alexander Lebed, the most popular politician in Russia.

Yeltsin interrupted the evening's scheduled television broadcasts to address the Russian people from the sanatorium where he is awaiting a heart operation. He accused Lebed of using his position to run a disguised campaign for the presidency. "I can no longer tolerate this situation," Yeltsin said, "and I am forced to relieve General Lebed of his position as secretary of the security council." He then dramatically signed the decree dismissing the general in front of the television cameras.

Lebed responded to the dismissal with a contemptuous insouciance. He said he was "not bothered in the slightest", and that he had "long since stopped being offended". But he warned that he was the only person trusted in Chechenia – "and not only in Chechenia," he added.

Lebed secured Yeltsin's re-election when he threw his support behind the Russian leader in the second round of the presidential ballot. But the general soon emerged as a potential rival. Tonight he vowed he would not contest the presidency "while Russia has a living president". The future of Russia now depends on the outcome of Yeltsin's operation. (→ November 5)

S	M	T	W	T	F	S
		1	2	3	4	5
6	7	8	9	10	11	12
13	14	15	16	17	18	19
20	21	22	23	24	25	26
27	28	29	30	31		

Tokyo, 20
The general election in Japan fails to produce a clear majority for the ruling Liberal Democratic party. Prime Minister Ryutaro Hashimoto remains in power, but his party will have to build a coalition.

Westminster, 20
Health ministers express sympathy for widow Diane Blood in her fight to be inseminated with her dead husband's sperm, and indicate they would favour a change in the fertilization law. The current law requires written consent from all sperm donors.

Eastern Zaire, 21
The UN reports that 220,000 Hutu refugees have left their camps and are fleeing into the hills in order to escape the conflict between the Zairean military and Tutsi guerrillas. (→ October 31)

London, 21
The Roman Catholic Church enters the political arena by issuing advice to Catholics voting in the next general election. Some claim the advice shows a bias towards Labour.

Nicaragua, 21
Right winger Arnoldo Aleman, the ex-mayor of Managua, claims victory in the Nicaraguan elections against Sandinista leader Daniel Ortega. (→ November 3)

London, 22
Sarah Holt and Sophie Bird – two young women jailed for contempt of court after they refused to testify against a man who terrorized them – are set free after one week in jail.

Zurich, 22
Switzerland admits that assets of Polish Holocaust victims were used to compensate Swiss nationals for property lost to communist Poland.

Tokyo, 22
Copper trader Yasuo Hamanaka, accused in June by his employers, Sumitomo Corp., of causing £1.2 billion in losses through unauthorized trading, is arrested on forgery charges.

Westminster, 25
The Home Secretary, Michael Howard, proposes radical changes in sentencing criminals, including minimum terms for repeat offenders.

STAMFORD BRIDGE, LONDON, SATURDAY 26
Chelsea bids farewell to Matthew Harding

Chelsea players, including player-manager Ruud Gullit (second right), clasp hands during the one-minute silence before kick-off.

Chelsea football club today paid tribute to millionaire vice-chairman Matthew Harding, who was killed four days ago in a helicopter crash. Before the kick-off of today's game against Tottenham, wreaths were laid in the centre circle of the field, and players joined hands for one minute's silence. Chelsea went on to win 3-1.

Four others died in the crash with Harding, who was on his way back from watching Chelsea play an away match against Bolton. Harding was a popular figure with both fans and players – "more like a supporter than a director", said player-manager Ruud Gullit – and had injected £25 million of his personal fortune into the club.

FLORIDA, FRIDAY 25
Shooting sets off Florida riot

The Florida city of St. Petersburg was rocked by rioting last night after a black motorist was shot dead by a white police officer. The motorist had been stopped for speeding.

The rioting began at the junction where the shooting took place. Police were bombarded with bottles and rocks. Later the trouble worsened. Shots were fired at police cars and petrol bombs were thrown. Firefighters were attacked when they arrived to control the fires.

Today the streets are calm. But the rioting is a brutal reminder of the continuing tension between many black residents and police in US cities. (→ November 14)

New York, Monday 21. Oscar-winning British animator Nick Park was inconsolable after he left the original models of his films' stars, Wallace and Gromit (above), in a taxi on Saturday. Luckily, it was only a close shave: the duo were safely returned to Mr. Park today.

O.J. trial drama recommences

Opening statements were heard today in what is effectively O.J. Simpson's second trial for the 1994 killing of Nicole Brown Simpson and Ronald Goldman. The victims' families are suing O.J. for wrongful death. With the laxer rules pertaining in a civil court and a new jury, they are hoping for a different outcome. (→ November 25)

O.J. Simpson, back in court for a civil trial.

Philip Lawrence's widow calls for moral crusade

Frances Lawrence with her son Lucien.

Frances Lawrence, the widow of Philip Lawrence, the London headmaster who was stabbed to death last year, has called for a national movement to banish violence and foster good citizenship. Four days after her husband's killer, 16-year-old Learco Chindamo, was found guilty at the Old Bailey, Mrs. Lawrence has published a manifesto aimed at reversing the "deterioration" of society. Her ideas are supported by Prime Minister John Major, Labour leader Tony Blair, and leaders of the Church of England and the Roman Catholic Church.

Mrs. Lawrence's manifesto calls for a moral crusade to be led by parents, teachers, and police. The status of teachers and police should be raised in society, she says, and children should be given lessons in good citizenship in school from an early age. Her other specific aims are a ban on the sale of combat knives, less violence on television, and promotion of family life.

John Major and Tony Blair have both backed Mrs. Lawrence's campaign, with Mr. Blair saying that her themes "cross traditional left and right boundaries". (→ December 5)

London, Tuesday 22. Alexander McQueen is named British designer of the year at the Lloyds Bank fashion awards. Last week, McQueen became designer-in-chief at Givenchy.

Chirac becomes a hero in Palestine after clash with Israeli security guards

French president Jacques Chirac today became the first foreign head of state to address the Palestinian Council, the parliament that rules the autonomous part of the West Bank and Gaza.

Chirac received a rapturous welcome in the West Bank after a public clash with Israeli security guards yesterday. On a visit to the holy sites of Jerusalem, the French president had been clearly angered by the guards who hemmed him in at every moment. At one point he shouted at their commander in English: "This is a provocation. Stop this now. What do you want, for me to go back to my plane and go home to France?"

Although Israeli prime minister Benyamin Netanyahu apologized for the incident, it dramatized the main thrust of Chirac's visit, which was to offer France's support to Palestinian leader Yassir Arafat in his dispute with Israel. Chirac called for the creation of an independent Palestinian state and a complete withdrawal of Israel from all the occupied territories, including East Jerusalem.

Young Palestinians welcome French president Jacques Chirac to Ramallah in the Palestinian-ruled part of the West Bank.

October

Islamabad, Pakistan, 27
Life in the Pakistan capital is brought to a standstill as Islamic militants demonstrating against Prime Minister Benazir Bhutto's government clash with security forces. (→ November 4)

Kabul, Afghanistan, 27
Forces opposed to the Taleban Islamic extremists bomb Kabul for the second night in a row.

Luxembourg, 28
EU foreign ministers agree to prohibit European companies from complying with US legislation that penalizes firms trading with Cuba, Iran, or Libya.

New York, 28
Newsweek magazine declares London is once again "the world's coolest city", thirty years after it was hailed as the centre of the Swinging Sixties.

London, 28
Lord Archer plans to introduce a bill in the House of Lords that would allow the sovereign's eldest child to inherit the throne, regardless of sex.

England and Wales, 28
Some of the worst gales since the great storm of 1987 sweep through England and Wales, leaving six dead and causing £150 million damage.

Atlanta, 28
Former Olympic security guard Richard Jewell is cleared by the FBI as a suspect in the July 27 Olympic bombing. Jewell says he plans to sue news organizations, which, he alleges, tried to pin the crime on him.

London, 29
Graham Swift wins the 1996 Booker Prize for his novel *Last Orders*. He was previously shortlisted for *Waterland*.

West Bank, 29
Palestinians riot at the funeral of a ten-year-old Arab boy allegedly killed by a Jewish settler.

Sao Paulo, Brazil, 31
A Brazilian airliner crashes into a residential neighbourhood in the city of Sao Paulo, killing at least 95 people.

London, 31
British scientists announce meteorite evidence of life on Mars that supports the claims publicized by NASA and American scientists in August.

HALIFAX, THURSDAY 31
Collapse of discipline creates schools crisis

Prime Minister John Major called on parents to keep a "proper perspective" as concern spread about severe discipline problems in state schools.

Today the Ridings School in Halifax was closed down because the local education authority felt disorder was so bad that the safety of staff and pupils could not be guaranteed. This follows the closing of the Manton junior school in Nottinghamshire on Monday for similar reasons.

In both schools, teachers have been at odds with governors and education authorities over the handling of disruptive children. The teachers at Manton school threatened to strike after one unruly pupil, Matthew Wilson, returned to normal classes. Staff at the Ridings School have voted unanimously for strike action unless 61 pupils are expelled.

VIENNA, TUESDAY 29
Jewish art plundered by Nazis auctioned

More than 8,000 paintings, drawings, and antiques stolen from Austrian Jews by the Nazis went up for auction in Vienna today. The proceeds will go to Holocaust survivors.

In an emotionally charged atmosphere, prices escalated well beyond the catalogue guide prices. The first day of the sale netted £8 million, four times the estimate for the entire two-day auction.

The art had been stored by the Austrian authorities ever since it was recovered after the Second World War. They have admitted that no effort was made to locate the original owners.

The bidding at the Jewish art auction proceeded in a tense and emotional atmosphere.

Thailand, Thursday 31. The Queen and Prince Philip, in Thailand on a state visit, are presented with home-woven silk by a Thai farmer during a tour of rural projects. Mr. Wang (right) expressed surprise at being asked to receive the royal couple at his smallholding, saying he had nothing worth showing.

GOMA, ZAIRE, THURSDAY 31

Million lives at risk as refugees flee battleground

Ethnic conflict in the east of Zaire, in central Africa, is threatening the lives of over a million Hutu refugees from Rwanda. A military offensive by rebel Tutsis has driven the refugees from their camps. Aid officials warn that, as the refugees flee, a cholera epidemic could erupt and food supplies may become cut off.

The present crisis broke out after Hutu extremists and Zairean government forces attacked Tutsis inside Zaire, trying to drive them out of areas where they have lived for more than two centuries. The Tutsis, backed by the Tutsi-dominated Rwandan government, counter-attacked and routed Zairean forces. This week they took one provincial capital, Bukavu, and threatened another, Goma.

Despite their precarious condition, the Hutu refugees are not returning to Rwanda. Many fear reprisals for the massacre of 500,000 Tutsis by Hutu extremists in 1994. (→ November 13)

Rwandan Hutu refugees set up a temporary camp as they trek across eastern Zaire in search of a secure place to settle.

Central London, Wednesday 30. Models stripped off in a chilly Covent Garden today to draw attention to a campaign against the wearing of fur coats.

CAIRO, EGYPT, TUESDAY 29

Two women rescued after 36 hours trapped under rubble

Late on Sunday, an apartment building collapsed in Heliopolis, a suburb of the Egyptian capital, Cairo. More than 150 people are believed to have been buried under the rubble.

Today, 36 hours after the disaster occurred, Samantha Miksche, 17, an Australian, and her Egyptian friend, Noha Fawzi, 19, were found alive by rescuers. They had been visiting the building with Miksche's mother to look at an apartment to rent. The mother is still missing, along with more than 100 other people.

The ruins of a Cairo apartment building that collapsed on Sunday.

BEIJING, WEDNESDAY 30

Chinese dissident is jailed

After a trial lasting three hours, a Chinese court today sentenced pro-democracy activist Wang Dan to 11 years in prison for "conspiring to subvert China's government".

Wang Dan, 27, was a student leader during the Tiananmen Square protest in 1989, and spent three years in jail after the protest was crushed. He has since continued to campaign for human rights and democracy. This is the crime for which he is punished.

Paris, Thursday 31. Marcel Carné, one of France's greatest film makers, died today aged 90. His masterpiece is *Les Enfants du Paradis*, a film made during the Nazi occupation of France in the Second World War.

November

S	M	T	W	T	F	S
					1	2
3	4	5	6	7	8	9
10	11	12	13	14	15	16
17	18	19	20	21	22	23
24	25	26	27	28	29	30

London, 2
Walker Ffyona Campbell admits that she never completed her famous around-the-world walk. She tells ITN that she took lifts from her back-up vehicle during the US leg of her journey.

London, 3
British Telecom announces it plans to take over US telephone company MCI Communications. It will be the largest-ever foreign takeover of a US company.

Managua, Nicaragua, 3
Supporters of the Sandinista party protest against their defeat in the recent national elections, claiming there was electoral fraud.

London, 4
Safety campaigners urge the government to ban giant fireworks after two deaths over the weekend. David Hattersley, a primary school headmaster and father of six, and Steve Timcke, a 34-year-old City trader, were killed when lighting fireworks.

Moscow, 4
US businessman Paul Tatum is shot dead in a Moscow underground station, probably by a Russian mafia hitman.

Southwark, London 4
The trial of seven conspirators charged with planning to steal hundreds of millions of pounds from bank cash machines begins. Kenneth Noye, the chief suspect in the "road rage" killing of Stephen Cameron last May, is believed to have been involved. Noye is still a fugitive.

Bangkok, 5
Singer Michael Jackson, on tour in Thailand, confirms that he is to have a child by 37-year-old nurse Debbie Rowe. (→ November 14)

Twickenham, 5
Phil de Glanville, 28, becomes the new captain of the England rugby team.

Deaths
November 1. Junius Jayawardene, former prime minister and president of Sri Lanka, aged 90.

November 3. Jean-Bedel Bokassa, former emperor of the Central African Republic, aged 75.

Flood from glacier sweeps across Iceland

A bridge swept away by the flood that erupted from Iceland's largest glacier.

A flood expected ever since the Loki volcano erupted last month beneath Europe's largest glacier burst across Iceland today. Prime Minister David Oddsson said the flooding was happening "on a much larger scale and much faster than we expected".

The volcanic eruption stopped on October 12, but by then it had melted a mass of ice that filled a vast lake under the glacier. Today, the water burst free and washed across the plains to the ocean. Fortunately, the area in the path of the flood had been evacuated, but roads, bridges, and power lines were swept away. The damage will cost millions of pounds to repair.

ISLAMABAD, MONDAY 4

Bhutto ousted by Pakistani president

The president of Pakistan, Farook Leghari, today dismissed the country's prime minister, Benazir Bhutto, and dissolved the national assembly. Army units surrounded Ms. Bhutto's official residence and occupied television and radio stations.

Ms. Bhutto has been severely criticized for alleged corruption and her failure to cope with the country's growing financial problems.

The president promised that fresh elections would be held within three months, but some observers believe a period of military rule is a more likely outcome of the crisis.

Benazir Bhutto, ousted Pakistani leader.

New York, Sunday 3. Runners in the New York City Marathon cross the Verrazano bridge. The men's race was won by Italian policeman Giacomo Leone.

LONDON, FRIDAY 1

Gazza selection met with anger

The announcement that footballer Paul Gascoigne will play for England in a World Cup qualifying match next week has caused a public outcry. Two weeks ago, Gascoigne's wife Sheryl was photographed with injuries that she had apparently sustained in a row with the footballer. Women's groups argue that his selection sends out the message that wife beating is acceptable. England's coach Glen Hoddle, a staunch Christian, today defended his choice, saying that, while he does not condone Gascoigne's behaviour, he accepts "that people are human".

Divers find sunken palace of Cleopatra

French marine archaeologists exploring beneath the Mediterranean Sea have discovered the remains of the royal district of ancient Alexandria, where Cleopatra and Mark Antony carried on their famous love affair more than 2,000 years ago.

Frank Goddio, the leader of the archaeologists, told reporters today: "It was a fantastic feeling diving on the remains of the city. To think when I touched a statue or sphinx, Cleopatra might have done the same."

The royal zone of Alexandria sank under the sea after an earthquake and tidal wave in AD335. It lies in the eastern harbour of modern Alexandria.

Ancient remains under the Mediterranean.

WASHINGTON, DC, WEDNESDAY 6

Clinton wins second White House term

The Clinton family savours a moment of triumph in Little Rock, Arkansas, as the president's election victory is confirmed.

The 1996 presidential election had long looked like a one-horse race, and so it proved to be when Americans went to the polls yesterday. President Clinton became the first Democrat since Franklin D. Roosevelt to win a second term in the White House.

Clinton fell just short of his goal of an absolute majority of the popular vote, taking 49 per cent, as against 41 per cent for Republican Bob Dole, and 8 per cent for Ross Perot. Clinton scored especially well with women, drawing 55 per cent of the female vote.

It was a day of triumph for the president, but not for Democrats in general. Clinton will again face a Republican-led Congress. Indeed, in the Senate the Republican majority even increased by one seat. Notable Republican victors were Jesse Helms in North Carolina and 93-year-old Strom Thurmond in South Carolina.

The day's most depressing statistic was voter turnout. Only 49 per cent of Americans bothered to vote, the lowest figure since 1924.

US, WEDNESDAY 6

Citizen initiatives call for change

As well as electing their representatives this week, voters across the US have also been responding to hotly contested ballot measures.

California was the site of two of the most notable results. By a substantial majority, Californians approved an initiative banning affirmative action on grounds of race or sex. They also voted to allow the medical use of marijuana. A similar initiative was approved in Arizona.

In Florida, a proposition limiting the state's ability to impose new taxes won an overwhelming majority. Voters in Colorado, however, rejected a proposal to add a new clause to the state constitution giving parents the right to "direct and control" their children's education.

Voters make their choice in Houston.

MOSCOW, TUESDAY 5

Yeltsin's heart surgery declared a success

Russian president Boris Yeltsin, aged 65, today underwent seven hours of gruelling heart-bypass surgery in a Moscow hospital. The operation was more complex than expected. Yeltsin needed five heart bypasses and his heart was stopped for 68 minutes.

Tonight, the Russian president is in intensive care and attached to an artificial respirator, but his condition is described as "stable". The US heart specialist who consulted on the operation, Michael DeBakey, said it was a total success. "President Yeltsin will be able to return to his office and carry out his duties in a normal fashion," Dr. DeBakey predicted.

President Yeltsin with Dr. Renat Akchurin, the head of the surgical team.

CAPE CANAVERAL, THURS. 7

Spacecraft blasts off for the Red Planet

A spacecraft lifted off from Cape Canaveral in Florida today, starting on a 700-million-km (435-million-mile) journey to Mars. The Global Surveyor should reach Mars next September. It will spend one Martian year – 687 earth days – in orbit, studying the Red Planet's atmosphere and mapping its surface features.

The Global Surveyor is the first of three Mars missions planned for this year, two of them American and one Russian. (→ November 18)

The race for the White House

ALL OBSERVERS AGREE that this was not a presidential election year to set the US on fire. The turnout of under 50 per cent of voters told its own story. Americans like a race with many dramatic twists, and one that goes to the wire. This was not it. President Bill Clinton led in the opinion polls from the start of the year and, riding the wave of a buoyant economy, never really looked as if he was going to lose.

Hot contest

The battle for the Republican nomination was probably the hottest phase of the political year. Once the backers of Steve Forbes and Pat Buchanan lost the Republican debate to the cautious Bob Dole, politics was squeezed into the centre ground.

At the start of the year Republicans had hopes that the Whitewater case and "Filegate" might sink the White House in scandal. But, despite a steady trickle of revelations, little of the dirt stuck. A last-minute scandal about possibly illegal foreign contributions to the Clinton campaign fund came far too late to have much effect.

Campaign winner

Republicans complained that the president stole their ideas and their policies. But responding to clear messages from a conservative, security-conscious electorate was a ploy that worked for Bill Clinton. He slashed welfare, took credit for budget cuts, got tough on crime, and adopted the family as the focus of his campaign. Dole was left pushing a 15 per cent cut in income tax as his sole big policy.

As a campaigner, Bob Dole was cruelly accident-prone. When he fell off a stage in Chico, California, it seemed a symbol of his performance. Some felt they would rather vote for Elizabeth Dole than for her husband. Bill Clinton, meanwhile, campaigned with his customary panache.

Clinton achieved a solid victory – almost half the national vote. However, the re-elected president faced plenty of problems. He once again confronted a Republican-dominated Congress, and scandals old and new still hung in the air. But 1996 was Bill Clinton's year.

The incumbent: President Clinton signs a bill raising the minimum wage by 20 per cent.

The challenger: Bob Dole in Montana shortly before clinching the Republican nomination.

Running mate: Dole's partner Jack Kemp.

Running mate: Confident Al Gore (centre).

Family: The Clintons rafting in Wyoming.

The Republican candidates

Ex-governor Lamar Alexander pulled out of the race in March.

Pat Buchanan came closest to threatening Dole's candidacy.

Steve Forbes campaigned on a 17-per-cent flat-tax platform.

The winner: Bill Clinton receives a warm welcome in St. Louis, Missouri. He remained popular throughout his campaign.

Wife: Hillary Clinton performs for US troops stationed in Bosnia.

Wife: Elizabeth Dole with husband Bob on his 73rd birthday.

S	M	T	W	T	F	S
					1	2
3	4	5	6	7	8	9
10	11	12	13	14	15	16
17	18	19	20	21	22	23
24	25	26	27	28	29	30

Moscow, 10
Thirteen people are killed and 16 wounded when a remote-controlled bomb explodes at a cemetery. The incident, thought to be an act of mafia vengeance, is the worst gangland killing in Russia in recent years.

Aberdeen, Maryland, 10
Fifteen non-commissioned officers are suspended at a US Army training base after allegations of sexual harassment. The case raises questions about widespread sexual abuse in the US Army.

Westminster, 12
Prime Minister John Major says he will not accept a European Court of Justice verdict obliging Britain to give most employees a 48-hour maximum working week and at least three weeks' paid holiday a year.

London, 13
The Securities and Investment Board criticizes pension firms for being slow to compensate people wrongly persuaded to quit company pensions for personal pensions. Only 6,277 out of 500,000 cases have been dealt with.

London, 14
The BBC announces that the quiz show *Mastermind* is to be phased out after running for 24 years.

St. Petersburg, Florida, 14
Riots erupt as a white police officer is cleared of the fatal shooting of an 18-year-old black man who had been stopped for speeding.

Coldstream, 15
The Stone of Scone, the ancient coronation stone of the Scottish kings, is returned from Westminster Abbey to Scotland, crossing the border at Coldstream. The stone was stolen by English King Edward I in 1296.

Westminster, 16
The Labour party changes its policy on Europe, pledging to hold a referendum before taking sterling into a single European currency.

Deaths
November 12. Don Kenyon, former Worcestershire cricket captain and opening batsman, aged 72.

November 15. Alger Hiss, prominent US diplomat accused of spying for Russia, in Manhattan, aged 92.

DELHI, TUESDAY 12
Worst-ever mid-air collision kills 350 people

A Saudi Arabian Boeing 747 collided with a Kazakh Airways Ilyushin 76 about 95 km (60 miles) outside the Indian capital, Delhi, today. All 312 passengers and crew on board the Boeing and 38 people on the Ilyushin are thought to have died – making it the world's third-worst air disaster, and the worst-ever mid-air collision.

A US Air Force cargo plane was flying into Delhi at the time. The captain described seeing "two fireballs…diverging from each other" as the planes fell from the sky.

Burning wreckage was littered over 10 km (6 miles) of farmland near the town of Charkhi Dadri. Bodies were carried away on carts as villagers aided rescue teams.

The jumbo jet was seven minutes out of New Delhi's international airport when the collision occurred. The incoming Kazakh flight was supposed to be flying 300 m (1,000 ft) above the jumbo. The Indian government has ordered a full inquiry.

The remains of the Ilyushin 76 that collided with a jumbo jet near Delhi.

AUSTRALIA, THURSDAY 14
Jackson weds for second time

Michael Jackson in Sydney last week.

Pop superstar Michael Jackson today wed Debbie Rowe, a 37-year-old nurse who is carrying his child. "Please respect our privacy and let us enjoy this exciting time" Jackson said in a written statement. The couple have known each other for 15 years, and it was announced last week that Rowe will give birth to the singer's child early in 1997. In 1994, Jackson wed Lisa Marie Presley, but that marriage collapsed earlier this year, with Presley citing "irreconcilable differences".

WESTMINSTER, MONDAY 11
Willetts roasted by Committee

David Willetts, the paymaster general and former Tory whip, was called before the House of Commons Standards and Privileges Committee today after a leaked 1994 memorandum apparently showed him trying to smother investigation of the Neil Hamilton cash-for-questions affair. Willetts was accused of deception by the Committee, which found that the evidence he gave to the inquiry contradicted his memo. (→ December 11)

London, Thursday 14. The film *First Wives Club* opens in Britain. Diane Keaton, Goldie Hawn, and Bette Midler play friends who band together to seek revenge after their rich husbands desert them.

Multi-national force planned to avert Zaire tragedy

A multi-national force is being organized to fly into eastern Zaire. The aim of the force will be to protect relief supplies for a million refugees threatened by starvation. Fighting between Tutsi rebels and Hutu militias is disrupting food aid.

Britain has agreed to join the multi-national force, which will be commanded by a Canadian officer, Lieutenant General Maurice Baril. Other countries that have promised to take part include the US, France, Italy, Spain, and South Africa.

The situation in eastern Zaire has led to severe doubts about the relief mission, however. There are fears that the multi-national force might be caught up in the Zairean conflict. The US has made it a condition of its participation that a ceasefire must first be agreed between Tutsi and Hutu fighters around the rebel-held town of Goma, through which aid supplies will be channelled. (→ November 18)

A young Hutu refugee in eastern Zaire, an area torn apart by ethnic conflict and the aftermath of genocidal massacres.

London, Sunday 10. Marjorie Proops, Britain's most famous agony aunt, died in hospital tonight. She is thought to have been 85 years old, although her age was a well-kept secret.

Al Fayeds win a round in citizenship fight

Mohamed Al Fayed, the owner of Harrods, and his brother Ali won a crucial round today in their battle for British citizenship. The Court of Appeal ruled that Home Secretary Michael Howard was wrong to refuse them citizenship without telling them on what grounds the decision had been made. Now he must do so and allow them a chance to reply.

Egyptian-born Mohamed Al Fayed told reporters: "I have lived here for 30 years without incurring so much as a parking ticket."

Pensioner turns down £2 million

An 89-year-old widow has written anonymously to the *Hull Daily Mail* saying that she has a winning National Lottery ticket worth over £2 million, but does not want to collect the money because "the fuss would finish me off". According to the widow's letter, the lottery ticket was bought by her husband shortly before he died. She says she wants the money to go to local hospitals – but if it remains uncollected it will be put into a lottery distribution fund that contributes to a range of causes.

Las Vegas, Sunday 10. In one of the greatest-ever upsets in boxing, Evander Holyfield defeated Mike Tyson by a technical knockout in the eleventh round last night. Holyfield, an 11-1 underdog, now holds the World Boxing Association heavyweight title.

November

London, 17
Jemima Khan, wife of former Pakistan cricket captain Imran Khan, gives birth to a son.

Western Australia, 17
Australian yachtsman David Dicks, 18, sails into Fremantle to become the youngest person to complete a non-stop circumnavigation of the world.

Westminster, 18
A motion calling for the banning of all handguns is defeated in the House of Commons. The government's measure allowing only .22 handguns kept in secure gun clubs is approved.

Washington, DC, 18
The CIA announces that one of its senior officers, Harold Nicholson, has been arrested on charges of spying for the Russians.

Vatican, 19
During a meeting with Cuban leader Fidel Castro in the Vatican, Pope John Paul II accepts an invitation to visit Cuba next year.

London, 19
Former England soccer manager Terry Venables announces he is to coach Australia's national soccer squad.

Los Angeles, 20
Pamela Anderson, star of the TV series *Baywatch*, separates from her husband, rock drummer Tommy Lee.

Leeds, 20
Rugby League authorities announce a World Club Championship to be played for the first time next year.

Hobart, Tasmania, 21
Martin Bryant is sentenced to life imprisonment for shooting 35 people dead at Port Arthur in April.

Hong Kong, 21
Thirty-nine people are killed and 80 injured in a fire in a high-rise building.

Comoros Islands, 23
An Ethiopian Airlines Boeing 767, hijacked between Addis Ababa and Nairobi, runs out of fuel off the Comoros Islands and crashes into the Indian Ocean. At least 123 people are killed. (→ November 25)

Deaths
November 19. Lord Bancroft, former head of the civil service, aged 73.

Telford, Sunday 17. Olympic medallist Tim Henman is now 27th in the world rankings. Today he beat Greg Rusedski to retain the UK championship.

BUCHAREST, MONDAY 18
Election ends Communist rule in Romania

Emil Constantinescu, victorious leader of the Romanian Democratic Convention.

Seven years after a revolution overthrew Romania's communist dictator, Nicolae Ceausescu, the grip of communists on the country has at last been shaken off. President Ion Iliescu, a top communist official under Ceausescu, has held power ever since the revolution. However, in the second round of elections held yesterday, he was defeated by a democratic opposition candidate, Emil Constantinescu.

Constantinescu led an alliance of anti-communist opposition groups. He called the result "a victory for millions of Romanians who lived through years of repression".

CALAIS, TUESDAY 19
Fire disaster closes the Channel Tunnel

A section of the Channel Tunnel was devastated by fire last night. The fire is believed to have started on a lorry that was being transported through the Tunnel on a freight train.

Thirty-three passengers and three train crew were rescued from the inferno. Six people were hospitalized, suffering from smoke inhalation.

The passengers were in a carriage at the front of the freight train. Today they described how they feared for their lives as smoke leaked into the carriage. They were trapped there for 20 minutes before help arrived. Jeff Waghorn, a lorry driver from Essex said: "It felt like a lifetime. You're lying there...wondering whether you're going to get out alive."

A limited freight service is restarting today, but Eurostar and Le Shuttle could remain suspended for several months. The Channel Tunnel Safety Authority, which is investigating the fire, may call for new safety measures before passenger services resume. The shutdown is costing Eurotunnel about £1 million a day. (→ November 26)

Bangalore, Saturday 23. Hindus protest against the holding of this year's Miss World beauty contest in Bangalore, India. Extremists had threatened to commit suicide at the event, but it went ahead today under tight security. Irene Skliva of Greece won the crown.

Refugees stream home to Rwanda

Hundreds of thousands of Hutu refugees set off for Rwanda from Mugunga camp in Zaire.

As advance parties of troops from a planned multi-national relief force arrived in central Africa at the end of last week, the Hutu refugees they had come to save from starvation began to leave their camps in Zaire and return to Rwanda. Today, a column of refugees 80 km (50 miles) long is filling the road from Goma in Zaire eastward to the Rwandan border. An estimated 400,000 refugees have crossed the border since last Friday.

The sudden abandonment of the refugee camps follows a rout of Hutu militias by Tutsi rebel forces backed by the Rwandan government. The surviving Hutu militiamen have fled, apparently intending to regroup in the Zairean interior. Freed from coercion by the militias, the majority of Hutus seemed eager to go home. Refugees interviewed by the press were confident they would not face retribution for the Hutu massacre of Tutsis in Rwanda in 1994, the starting point of the current crisis.

It seems certain that the deployment of the multi-national force will now not go ahead as originally conceived. Observers on the ground in Zaire are warning, however, that the refugee problem is far from resolved. The future of about half a million refugees remains in doubt, and the prospect of further fighting in the zone remains a potent threat to the humanitarian aid effort.

New York, Monday 18. Actor Daniel Day-Lewis (above) has married Rebecca Miller, the daughter of playwright Arthur Miller, it was announced today.

NEW YORK, TUESDAY 19

US stands alone in vetoing re-election of UN leader

At a meeting of the UN Security Council today, US representative Madeleine Albright vetoed a second four-year term for the current UN secretary-general, Boutros Boutros Ghali. All other 14 council members supported Boutros Ghali's re-election.

The US veto can be overruled by the UN General Assembly, but this is unlikely to happen. The UN needs the $1.4 billion that it is owed by the US. If the US does not get its way, it is unlikely to pay up. (→ December 13)

UN Secretary-General Boutros Boutros Ghali, hoping for a second term in office.

MOSCOW, MONDAY 18

Russian Mars probe lands in the Pacific

Russia's space programme is in disarray today after the Mars-96 spacecraft, launched from a site in Kazakhstan on Saturday, fell back to Earth and crashed into the Pacific Ocean.

Experts are still analyzing the cause of the failure, but it appears that booster rockets that should have propelled the craft deep into space failed to fire. More fundamentally, the setback is blamed on severe underfunding of the Russian space programme since the breakup of the Soviet Union. (→ December 4)

London, Wednesday 20. Westminster council today banned David Cronenberg's film *Crash* from cinemas in London's West End. The film features explicit sex scenes involving car-crash victims.

November

Minsk, Belarus, 25
The president of Belarus, Alexander Lukashenko, wins sweeping new powers in a referendum that moves the country closer to dictatorship.

Santa Monica, 25
In O.J. Simpson's civil trial for the wrongful deaths of his ex-wife, Nicole Brown Simpson, and Ronald Goldman, O. J. changes elements of his alibi, claiming he was in the shower at the time of the murders.

Wishaw, Scotland, 27
Five people have died and 100 are ill after an outbreak of food poisoning. Investigators are concentrating on cooked meat from a local butcher's as the source. (→ December 4)

Westminster, 27
Prime Minister John Major lays down conditions for a "lasting ceasefire" that would allow Sinn Fein leaders entry to the all-party talks on the future of Northern Ireland.

Henley, 28
British rower Steve Redgrave, who has won four Olympic gold medals, says he will compete in the next Olympics as part of a coxless four. Redgrave had earlier claimed that the Atlanta Games would be his last Olympics. (→ December 15)

Birmingham, 28
In a world-record event, Sir Simon Rattle conducts the largest symphony orchestra ever assembled – 2,845 schoolchildren performing *Let Music Live*, a piece composed specially for the occasion by Howard Blake.

Bethlehem, 29
Greek Orthodox churchmen claim a modern miracle, saying that a painting of Jesus in the Basilica of the Nativity in Bethlehem has begun weeping. The painting sits above a grotto said to mark the exact spot of Jesus's birth.

Cape Town, 29
Newly released documents reveal that South African government ministers approved a policy of killing black demonstrators who were protesting against apartheid in 1976.

Pale, Bosnia, 29
General Ratko Mladic, an indicted war criminal, formally resigns as head of the Bosnian Serb Army.

Death toll rises in hijacking disaster

The wreckage of the hijacked Ethiopian Airlines Boeing 767 juts out of the sea off the shore of the largest of the Comoros Islands.

The death toll in the crash of Ethiopian Airlines flight ET961 rose to 127 today, making this the deadliest hijacking in aviation history.

The airliner was hijacked on Saturday after taking off from Addis Ababa, Ethiopia. Three Ethiopians demanded that the plane fly to Australia and refused to allow the pilot to land at Nairobi, Kenya. The aircraft then headed for the Comoros Islands in the Indian Ocean.

The airliner ran out of fuel and crashlanded in the sea a few hundred metres from a holiday beach on Grand Comore. Passengers and crew were helped to safety by holiday makers, but only 52 people initially survived and four of those have since died. It is unclear whether any of the hijackers are among the survivors.

GLOUCESTER, FRIDAY 29
John West found hanged at home

The younger brother of serial killer Fred West was found dead at his home in Gloucester last night. John West, 54, hanged himself in his garage, replicating his brother Fred's suicide in 1995.

John West's death came near the end of his trial for the multiple rape of his niece – Fred West's daughter Anne Marie Davis – and another woman. Ms. Davis alleges that her uncle raped her 300 times at 25 Cromwell Street in Gloucester. The jury were to begin considering their verdict today.

Fred West tried to implicate his brother John in the Cromwell Street murders, but the jury in the rape trial was told that there was no evidence to suggest such an involvement.

London, Wednesday 27. Actor Michael Bentine died today, aged 74. He was one of the founders of the 1950s radio comedy series *The Goon Show*, and created a highly successful TV show, *It's a Square World*.

THE HAGUE, FRIDAY 29
War Crimes Tribunal gives first sentence

Drazen Erdemovic, 25, a former soldier in the Bosnian Serb Army became the first person to be sentenced by the War Crimes Tribunal in The Hague today. He was jailed for ten years for his part in the massacre of 1,200 Muslims in Srebrenica in 1995.

Erdemovic, a lance-corporal, was only a minor player in the genocidal acts of the Bosnia Serb Army. He confessed to being part of an execution squad that shot Muslims in groups of ten at a farm 70 km (45 miles) north of Srebrenica. Prosecutors say that they might not have uncovered the crime but for Erdemovic's confession.

WESTMINSTER, TUESDAY 26
Budget leak upstages tax cuts

Under pressure to produce a budget that would revive the government's fortunes before next year's general election, Chancellor of the Exchequer Kenneth Clarke today announced a 1p cut in income tax and raised tax thresholds by more than inflation.

The chancellor's upbeat speech was upstaged, however, by the revelation in yesterday's *Daily Mirror* that details of the budget had been leaked to the paper in advance. The *Mirror* chose not to publish the information, but an angry John Major has ordered MI5 to investigate the leak.

Kenneth Clarke on budget day.

Channel Tunnel, Tuesday 26. The first pictures were released today of the damage caused by last week's Channel Tunnel fire. Intense heat buckled rails and destroyed pipes and cables. A burnt-out freight shuttle wagon is still trapped in the Tunnel. (→ December 4)

BELGRADE, THURSDAY 28
Serbian protestors call for revolt

Protestors fill the streets of Belgrade.

Opposition groups in Serbia today called for the resignation of the Serbian president, Slobodan Milosevic. The demand came as crowds of anti-government protestors filled the streets of the capital, Belgrade, for the eleventh consecutive day.

The protests were sparked by the refusal of the government to accept the results of municipal elections that would have given the opposition control of Serbia's major cities. An electoral commission packed with government supporters declared the results invalid because of alleged "irregularities". (→ December 1)

PARIS, THURSDAY 28
Lorry drivers claim victory in French blockade

French lorry drivers today lifted their 12-day-old blockade of roads and ports after the French government and haulage companies made major concessions over pay, conditions and retirement benefits.

The lorry blockade had caused traffic chaos and threatened supplies of fresh foodstuffs to British supermarkets. Petrol stations across France ran dry as oil refineries were blockaded. At least a thousand British lorries were trapped by the dispute, especially around the Channel ports. British lorry owners will now be seeking compensation.

French drivers have won the right to retirement at 55, a ban on Sunday working, and tax breaks for companies that reduce working hours.

French lorries block the road outside an oil refinery near Marseilles in southern France.

OUTER SPACE, SATURDAY 30
Asteroid misses Earth, but is likely to return

The asteroid Toutatis passed within 5 million km (3 million miles) of the Earth this morning – near enough to raise again the spectre of a potential catastrophe. Toutatis is a lump of rock 5 km (3 miles) long, travelling at about 140,000 kmph (85,000 mph). If it hit the Earth, it would make a crater 50 km (30 miles) across and plunge the world into prolonged darkness as dust blotted out the sun.

Toutatis comes close to the Earth every four or five years. Scientists think a collision is highly unlikely for at least two centuries, but the asteroid's path is not entirely predictable.

December

Belgrade, 1
Up to 100,000 people take to the streets, demanding the resignation of President Slobodan Milosevic. The government threatens a crackdown on the demonstrations, claiming they are organized by the opposition.

Nottingham, 2
Two teenage girls are convicted of manslaughter and sentenced to two years in detention for the killing of 13-year-old schoolgirl Louise Allen during a fight in April.

London, 4
Eurostar resumes its passenger service, two weeks after the Channel Tunnel fire. The first train leaves Waterloo without any passengers.

Cape Canaveral, 4
NASA's Mars Pathfinder lander blasts off, beginning its journey to the Red Planet. It is due to touch down on Mars on July 4, 1997.

Westminster, 5
Prime Minister John Major and Labour leader Tony Blair engage in a row in the Commons over leaked Tory proposals to cut war widow benefits and compensation for disabled former servicemen.

London, 5
A couple claiming to be social workers allegedly attempt to abduct nine-year-old Lucien Lawrence, the son of murdered headmaster Philip Lawrence, from his home in Ealing.

London, 5
The Duchess of Kent – one of the most popular members of the royal family – is suffering from chronic fatigue syndrome (commonly known as ME), her office announces.

Zimbabwe, 5
England cricketers suffer one of their most humiliating defeats when Mashonaland, the weakest cricketing nation in the world, beats them with one day to spare.

London, 5
Sifiso Masango, the ten-year-old Zulu boy who was sent back to his natural parents in South Africa in January at the courts' insistence, returns to Britain. He will live in London with the woman who brought him up.

Tory majority at an end as MP withdraws support

Sir John Gorst, Conservative MP for Hendon North, has announced he is withdrawing his support from the government. This move finally wipes out John Major's majority in the House of Commons, which has been dwindling throughout the year.

Sir John is protesting at the government's failure to keep open a full-time accident unit at Edgware General hospital, a matter of great importance to his constituents. (→ December 12)

Clinton chooses woman as his secretary of state

UN ambassador Madeleine Albright

The US ambassador to the United Nations, Madeleine Albright, seems almost certain to become America's first woman secretary of state. President Clinton has nominated her to replace Warren Christopher. The appointment still requires the approval of Congress, but this is expected to be little more than a formality.

Ms. Albright is the daughter of a Czech diplomat who sought asylum in the US when the communists took over Czechoslovakia in 1948. During her four years as ambassador to the UN, she has gained a reputation as a blunt and outspoken advocate of American interests. She is expected to be more hawkish in her approach than her low-key predecessor.

Teacher saved children in machete attack

Horret Campbell, on trial for a machete attack on a Wolverhampton infants school.

At Stafford crown court today, a jury heard how nursery teacher Lisa Potts tried to defend a group of infants from an attacker wielding a machete.

The prosecution alleges that the defendant, Horret Campbell, aged 33, entered the grounds of St. Luke's Church of England school in Blakenhall, Wolverhampton, last July. He attacked 20 children who were enjoying a teddy bears' picnic, injuring three infants, three mothers, and the nursery teacher.

Ms. Potts described how the infants clung to her as she tried to shield them from Campbell's blows: "Some were holding on to my skirt and some of them went underneath. They were hiding with fright... The man was in front of me and came at me with the machete. I put up my arm to protect my face and he lashed out at me."

Ms. Potts suffered cuts to her head, arm, hand, and back. The judge, Mr. Justice Sedley, praised the teacher's "great unselfishness".

The court was told that police found newspaper cuttings about mass murderers such as Thomas Hamilton and Martin Bryant on Campbell's bedroom wall. (→ December 9)

London, Sunday 1. Granada Television launches an adaptation of *Moll Flanders*, starring Alex Kingston (above). The screening of Daniel Defoe's bawdy classic coincides with Heritage Secretary Virginia Bottomley's call for a crackdown on TV sex and violence.

WORCESTERSHIRE, MONDAY 2
Driver stabbed to death after "road rage" chase

Lee Harvey, aged 25, has died in what appears to be a "road rage" killing. He was stabbed 15 times, apparently by a passenger from a car that he had overtaken on the A38. The murder took place near the village of Alvechurch, Worcestershire, where Mr. Harvey lived. His fiancée, Tracey Andrews, who was in the car with him, was also injured. (→ December 8)

Northern Russia, Friday 6. An estimated 30,000 reindeer are at risk from starvation. Blizzards last month have left their winter grazing areas covered in ice.

WASHINGTON, DC, TUESDAY 3
Frozen lake found in crater on Moon

American scientists believe they have discovered a frozen lake at the bottom of a crater on the dark side of the Moon. The evidence comes from the Pentagon-financed Clementine satellite that orbited the Moon in 1994. The Moon was previously believed to be absolutely dry.

Astronomer Anthony Cook of the Griffith Observatory in Los Angeles emphasized the importance of the discovery for a future Moon colony: "With water there you could grow plants, grow food, and make your own fuel and air," he said.

PARIS, TUESDAY 3
Terrorists bomb crowded Paris underground train

Ambulances outside the Port Royal station after the bomb explosion this evening.

Algerian Islamic terrorists are believed to be responsible for a bomb explosion that tore through a carriage of an underground train in Paris this evening. The explosion occurred at 6:05 p.m., as the train, packed with commuters, was pulling into Port Royal station. At least two people have been killed and 20 injured.

The bombing was described by President Jacques Chirac as "a barbaric and terrorist act". It exactly resembles an attack on St. Michel station last year in which eight people died.

London, Monday 2. The first book is placed on the shelves of the new British Library at St. Pancras. The controversial building has cost £511 million so far, and is set to open in one year's time.

LANARKSHIRE, WEDNESDAY 4
Food poisoning death toll rises

The number of fatalities in the Scottish food poisoning outbreak rose to seven today with the death of a 74-year-old man. The outbreak began in mid-November, and has been traced to cooked meat supplied by award-winning butchers John M. Barr & Son, of Wishaw, Lanarkshire. The meat was infected with the virulent *E. coli 0157* bacteria, which can be fatal to children and the elderly.

There has been criticism of delays and confusion in informing the public after the source of the infection was identified. Over 160 people have so far been infected. (→ December 14)

KENSINGTON, MONDAY 2
Drink row unseats old campaigner Sir Nicholas Scott

Sir Nicholas Scott puts a brave face on his rejection by local Tory party members.

Sir Nicholas Scott, MP for Chelsea, last night lost his fight to contest the new seat of Kensington and Chelsea at next year's general election. A mass meeting of local party members in Kensington Town Hall voted by 509 votes to 439 to seek a new candidate.

Sir Nicholas claimed to have given up alcohol after a drink-driving conviction in March, but was found lying in a gutter during the Conservative party conference two months ago. He insists that this was not the result of drinking. Sir Nicholas described the deselection as "a sad moment". He has been an MP for 30 years.

December

Redditch, 8
Reports suggest that Tracey Andrews, fiancée of alleged "road rage" victim Lee Harvey, may be a suspect in the murder inquiry. She is in hospital, under police guard. (→ December 19)

Stafford, 9
Horret Campbell is found guilty on seven counts of attempted murder for his machete attack on an infants school in Wolverhampton last July.

Westminster, 10
The government announces an inquiry into Gulf War syndrome after claiming it had been misled by civil servants about the exposure of troops to pesticides.

Baghdad, Iraq, 10
Iraq resumes oil exports for the first time since their invasion of Kuwait six years ago. Under a UN plan, Iraq will use oil revenues to buy food and medicine.

Sharpeville, South Africa, 10
President Mandela signs South Africa's post-apartheid constitution in Sharpeville, site of a 1960 massacre of unarmed black demonstrators.

West Bank, 11
Two Jewish settlers, Etta and Ephraim Tzur, are shot dead when their car is ambushed by Palestinian gunmen.

London, 11
John McCarthy, whose half-brother was killed in the 1989 Hillsborough football disaster, is awarded £201,000 damages by the High Court.

Barnsley, 12
Labour candidate Jeff Ennis wins the Barnsley East by-election with a 13,181 majority. The result effectively makes the Tory government a minority administration.

Lanarkshire, 14
A twelfth person dies in the food poisoning epidemic that started from John Barr butcher's in Wishaw. It is now one of the world's worst outbreaks of infection with the *E. coli 0157* bacterium.

Deaths
December 9. Mary Leakey, the discoverer of some of the world's earliest homonid fossils, in Nairobi, Kenya, aged 83.

MAIDA VALE, SUNDAY 8
Plaque honours murdered head

On the first anniversary of the death of murdered headmaster Philip Lawrence, his nine-year-old son Lucien unveiled a commemorative plaque outside St. George's Roman Catholic School, Maida Vale, today. Among those present at the ceremony were the Duchess of Kent, the Archbishop of Westminster, Cardinal Basil Hume, and Home Secretary Michael Howard. The Duchess of Kent described Mr. Lawrence as "a shining example" to everyone.

The Duchess of Kent and Lucien Lawrence.

NEW YORK, FRIDAY 13
Ghanaian Annan takes over as new head of UN

The United Nations Security Council today unanimously voted to support Kofi Annan, head of UN peacekeeping, as the next secretary-general. He replaces Boutros Boutros Ghali, who was prevented from serving a second term by a US veto.

Mr. Annan, a 58-year-old Ghanaian who has come up through the ranks of the UN, originally lacked the support of France, who preferred the Egyptian Boutros Ghali or a candidate from francophone Africa. They dropped their veto when they saw that Mr. Annan enjoyed widespread support. The appointment will be ratified next week by the General Assembly.

London, Wednesday 11. Willie Rushton, one of Britain's best-loved comedians and satirists, died today after a heart operation. He was 59 years old. Rushton was a founder of the magazine *Private Eye*. He also appeared regularly as a storyteller on BBC children's television.

LONDON, THURSDAY 12
Sexy Spice Girls vote Tory and claim Thatcher as soul sister

The Spice Girls, the all-girl pop band currently topping the singles charts in 28 countries, are offering their support to the Tory party's Euro-sceptics.

According to an interview in *The Spectator* magazine, the Spice Girls are opposed to a single European currency and reject Labour's tax policies. Says 24-year-old Geri: "We Spice Girls are true Thatcherites. Thatcher was the first Spice Girl, the pioneer of our ideology – Girl Power."

The Spice Girls have bucked the trend of pop bands endorsing Tony Blair's Labour party.

WESTMINSTER, WEDNESDAY 11

Willetts resigns after damning criticism

David Willetts resigned today as paymaster general, after the publication of a highly critical report by a Commons committee investigating parliamentary sleaze. The Standards and Privileges Committee accused Willetts of "dissembling" in his evidence to the committee, and said it could not accept much of his written or oral evidence as accurate. Willetts resigned minutes after the report was published, although he maintained that he had always told the truth.

The committee had been investigating Willetts's part in an apparent attempt to stifle a 1994 Commons inquiry into allegations that Tory MP Neil Hamilton had accepted money for asking parliamentary questions. Willetts, then a junior whip, had allegedly suggested the possibility of exploiting the Tory majority on the relevant committee to push through a favourable judgement.

The report of the Standards and Privileges Committee condemned Willetts's behaviour in 1994, but said the original offence had been "substantially aggravated" by his lack of candour in giving evidence about it.

The loss of Willetts, seen as a high-flier in the Tory party, is another body blow to the government.

London, Wednesday 11. The High Court today ordered Morrissey (above), leader of The Smiths, to pay £1 million to drummer Mike Joyce, who has claimed an equal share in the group's profits.

NEW YORK, TUESDAY 10

Princess's new clothes create a sensation

Diana, Princess of Wales, caused a stir in New York last night when she arrived at a fashion gala wearing one of the latest lingerie-style dresses. The midnight-blue silk gown was designed specially for the princess by Britain's John Galliano, the new head designer at Christian Dior.

The ball was held to mark the fiftieth anniversary of Dior's New Look, and the princess's stunning entrance was a coup for both Galliano and Dior. The dress, a gift to the princess, is estimated to be worth £15,000.

The princess's sensational slip-style dress.

LONDON, FRIDAY 13

McLibel case staggers to a close

David Morris and Helen Steel, the environmental campaigners who took on McDonald's.

After two and a half years, Britain's longest ever libel trial, known as the "McLibel" case, ended at the High Court, London, today. McDonald's, the fast-food chain, was suing two almost penniless campaigners, David Morris and Helen Steel, for claiming in a leaflet that the company harmed the environment and exploited cheap Third World labour. Morris and Steel conducted their own defence, producing an array of detailed evidence to support their views. The judgement is not expected until next year.

HONG KONG, WEDNESDAY 11

Next Hong Kong leader is chosen

Shipping tycoon Tung Chee-Hwa was today selected to lead Hong Kong out of colonial rule as its chief executive. A 400-member committee, chosen by Beijing, gave Mr. Tung 320 votes. Two other candidates, both prominent Hong Kong figures, shared the remaining votes. Mr. Tung was already seen as China's man, following a pointed handshake from Chinese president Jiang Zemin in January.

Outside the hall where the vote took place, 29 pro-democracy protestors were arrested for trying to disrupt what they called a "phoney election". Mr. Tung will take over leadership of Hong Kong from British governor Chris Patten on July 1, 1997.

WESTMINSTER, TUESDAY 10

Peers support Archer's Bill

Lord Archer—seeking to change succession.

The House of Lords yesterday voted in favour of Lord Archer of Weston-super-Mare's bill, which would allow women equal rights of succession to the throne. Peers voted 74 to 53 to allow Lord Archer to approach the Queen, asking her permission to bring the bill before Parliament. If the bill is enacted, Princess Anne would overtake Prince Andrew in succession to the throne, and Prince William's first-born child would become monarch regardless of its sex.

December

Washington, DC, 16
US aerospace companies Boeing and McDonnell Douglas announce a £28 billion merger. The new company, which will dominate world aircraft production, poses a serious challenge to Europe's Airbus Industrie.

Honduras, 17
Delayed reports from a remote region of the country reveal that a meteorite, thought to be only 30 cm (1 ft) wide, crashed to earth two weeks ago, leaving a 50-m (165-ft) crater.

Grozny, 17
The Red Cross pulls all foreign staff out of Chechenia following the deaths of five nurses who were shot in their sleep by masked gunmen.

Strasbourg, 17
The European Court of Human Rights rules that Ernest Saunders, the disgraced former Guinness chairman, was not given a fair trial when he was found guilty of fraud in 1986.

Bologna, Italy, 19
Prosecutors charge Renault Williams team owner Frank Williams with the manslaughter of racing driver Ayrton Senna. Senna died in a crash in 1994, and prosecutors allege that there was a fault with his car's steering.

London, 20
Emma Gifford, daughter of a millionaire Rank Organisation executive, is given three years' probation for killing her newborn baby. Ms. Gifford admits to smothering her child hours after she gave birth alone in her flat.

London, 21
Russell Christie, the younger brother of Olympic sprinter Linford Christie, is stabbed to death on Portobello Road. Simon Williams, aged 32, is charged with the murder.

Deaths
December 16. Quentin Bell, nephew and biographer of novelist Virginia Woolf, in Sussex, aged 86.

December 17. Ruby Murray, 1950s singing star, from liver failure in a Devon hospital, aged 61.

December 20. Carl Sagan, American astronomer who popularized science with his 1980 TV series *Cosmos*, in Seattle, aged 62.

WORCESTERSHIRE, THURS. 19
Fiancée charged in "road rage" murder case

Tracey Andrews, aged 27, has been charged with the murder of her fiancé, Lee Harvey, near Alvechurch, Worcestershire, three weeks ago.

The killing was at first believed to be the result of a "road rage" attack. Ms. Andrews told police and the media that she and Mr. Harvey had been pursued by a Ford Sierra, and that one of the occupants of the Sierra stabbed Mr. Harvey to death.

The police say they have found no evidence of a car chase. They claim that Ms. Andrews stabbed her fiancé after a violent row. Ms. Andrews has attempted suicide and is being detained in a secure psychiatric hospital. She insists that the original "road rage" story is true. (→ December 23)

LONDON, SUNDAY 15
Hill and Redgrave take BBC honours

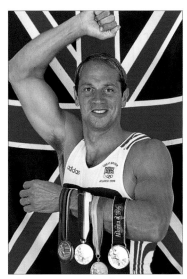

Olympic rower Steve Redgrave.

In the BBC's *Sports Review of the Year* last night, BBC viewers voted racing driver Damon Hill Sports Personality of the Year. Hill won the Formula One World Championship in the final race of the season in October. Rower Steve Redgrave, four times Olympic-gold winner, was runner-up for the BBC award. Retired boxer Frank Bruno won a lifetime achievement award.

LONDON, THURSDAY 19
Duke blunders as he defends gun users

Duke of Edinburgh: Caused outrage by suggesting guns are no more lethal than cricket bats.

The Duke of Edinburgh has outraged Dunblane campaigners and caused a furore with comments yesterday that gun club members are no more dangerous than any other sports persons.

Speaking on BBC Radio 5, Prince Philip said: "I mean, if a cricketer, for instance, suddenly decided to go into a school and batter a lot of people to death...are you going to ban cricket bats?" Anne Pearson, Dunblane anti-gun spokesperson, said she was sickened by the comments: "He has no idea what we are campaigning for."

Paris, Thursday 19. Italian actor Marcello Mastroianni died today, aged 73. He often played jaded Latin lovers, and will be remembered as the dissipated journalist in Federico Fellini's *La Dolce Vita* (above).

LIMA, PERU, THURSDAY 19

Guerrillas threaten to kill hostages

A band of guerrillas belonging to a small Marxist group, the Tupac Amaru Revolutionary Movement, is holding several hundred people hostage at the Japanese embassy in Lima, the capital of Peru. They have threatened to begin shooting hostages unless Peru's president, Alberto Fujimori, agrees to speak to them face-to-face.

About 500 diplomats, officials, politicians and Japanese businessmen were attending a reception in a tent in the embassy grounds on Tuesday evening when the guerrillas infiltrated the party disguised as waiters. They took over the gathering, letting off explosives and exchanging fire with police. They later released 170 women and elderly hostages. Those still in the guerrillas' hands include 18 ambassadors, the heads of several major Japanese companies, and the president of Peru's supreme court.

A guerrilla spokesperson said: "What we are asking is the liberation of all of our comrades, who are being

Heavily armed security forces surround the Japanese embassy where the hostages are held.

mistreated and tortured in the dungeons of the various prisons." He claimed the guerrillas were ready to die, and to kill all the hostages.

President Fujimori is known for taking a tough line with guerrillas. He has already said he will refuse to bend to their demands. (→ December 22)

Chelsea, Monday 16. Sir Laurens van der Post, explorer, writer, and mystic, died today, aged 90. Born in South Africa and author of 26 books, he influenced Prince Charles's spiritual views.

WESTMINSTER, TUESDAY 17

Tories accused of cheating in fishing vote

LONDON, TUESDAY 17

Now it's the £2 in your pocket

The £2 coin, in circulation next November.

The Royal Mint today unveiled a £2 coin, which will be jingling in purses and pockets next winter. It is the first British coin in two colours, the cupro-nickel centre contrasting with a nickel-brass outer band.

The design on the back of coin is by a Norfolk art teacher, Bruce Rushin, whose entry was judged the best of 1,200 submitted in an open competition. The design is intended to symbolize the progress of technology through British history.

Los Angeles, Sunday 15. Madonna arrives at the LA premiere of her much-hyped new film, *Evita*. The pop star is said to have begged director Alan Parker for the lead in his musical, and in the course of the film came to bear a striking resemblance to Eva Peron.

Deputy Prime Minister Michael Heseltine

The government is shrugging off accusations that it cheated in a crucial vote on fisheries policy last night. The opposition claims that Tory whips abused the pairing system, under which MPs from opposed parties agree not to vote, thus enabling them to be absent during key votes without affecting the result. The whips paired three Tory MPs with both Labour and Liberal Democrat MPs, in effect cutting the opposition vote by three. The government ended up with a majority of 11, allowing Michael Heseltine to say: "Whatever happened, we would have won."

S	M	T	W	T	F	S
1	2	3	4	5	6	7
8	9	10	11	12	13	14
15	16	17	18	19	20	21
22	23	24	25	26	27	28
29	30	31				

Bulawayo, Zimbabwe, 22
The first Test of the cricket series between England and Zimbabwe ends in a draw with the scores level.

Oxford, 23
Tracey Andrews, charged with the murder of her fiancé Lee Harvey, is released on bail by Oxford Crown Court. The police opposed bail.

Hornsea, Yorkshire, 23
Cara Weatherstone, aged 6, is killed by electrocution when she switches on the family Christmas-tree lights.

Moscow, 23
President Boris Yeltsin returns to the Kremlin to resume his duties after his heart-bypass operation. He claims to be "ready for battle".

Frankfurt, 24
A 49-year-old woman blows herself up during a Christmas Eve service in a crowded church in the Frankfurt suburb of Sindlingen, killing herself and two other people.

Britain, 25
The BBC comedy show *Only Fools and Horses* tops the TV Christmas ratings, attracting an estimated 18.7 million viewers. Overall, the BBC claims to have had eight out of ten top-rated shows on Christmas Day.

Gaza, 26
Palestinian leader Yassir Arafat tells a closed session of the Palestinian Legislative Council that an agreement on Israeli withdrawal from the town of Hebron will be signed within a week. Hebron is the last West Bank town still under Israeli military rule.

Seoul, South Korea, 28
A wave of strikes paralyzes South Korea as trade unionists protest against a draconian new labour law. The law was rushed through parliament in a dawn sitting, in the absence of opposition deputies.

Guatemala City, 29
Left-wing guerrillas and the president of Guatemala, Alvaro Arzu, sign a peace accord to end the country's 36 years of civil war.

Aveley, Essex, 29
William and Jill Willis, both aged 58, die after falling into a frozen lake while trying to rescue their labrador, Tara. The dog escapes unharmed.

White Christmas cheers punters

A light sprinkling of pre-dawn snow on London this morning brought a smile to thousands of punters who had bet on a white Christmas, and gloom to bookmakers, faced with paying out in excess of £100,000.

According to Ladbrokes, it was the first time for 20 years that there had been an official white Christmas declared in the capital. Other cities across the country also experienced light falls of snow, and more snow is predicted to be on the way.

Shilton breaks the 1,000 barrier

Former England goalkeeper Peter Shilton played his one thousandth league football match today, a feat unprecedented in soccer history.

Shilton's career began at Leicester City 31 years ago. Now aged 47, he appears for Leyton Orient in the Third Division. In between times, he won 125 England caps and two European Cup winners' medals.

As so often before, Shilton kept a clean sheet today, as Leyton beat Brighton Hove Albion 2-0.

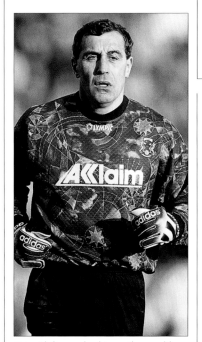

Peter Shilton makes his one thousandth English league football appearance.

British nurses face murder charge

Yvonne Gilford, the Australian nurse who was murdered this month in Dhahran.

Two British nurses have today been charged with the murder of an Australian colleague, Yvonne Gilford, in Saudi Arabia. Lucille McLauchlan from Dundee, aged 33, and 41-year-old Deborah Parry from Birmingham were arrested by Saudi police after allegedly being caught using the dead nurse's credit cards.

The murder took place at the King Fahd Military Medical Complex in Dharhan on December 11. If found guilty of premeditated murder by a Saudi court, the two British nurses could be publicly beheaded.

Britain, Tuesday 31. *Independence Day* **was the highest grossing film in the UK in 1996, taking more than £35 million at the box office.** *Toy Story* **and** *Babe* **were the second and third highest earners this year.**

Northern Ireland on the brink of return to sectarian warfare

A booby-trap bomb exploded in the Ardoyne area of north Belfast this lunchtime, seriously injuring Eddie Copeland, a prominent Republican alleged by Unionists to be an IRA "godfather". The bomb was planted under the driver's seat of Copeland's car. Although no organization has admitted responsibility for the bomb attack, it is almost certain to be the work of Unionist paramilitaries.

The bombing is thought to be a response to Friday's wounding of a policeman at the Royal Belfast Hospital for Sick Children. Two IRA gunmen shot the policeman while he was guarding the Unionist politician Nigel Dodds, who was at the bedside of his six-year-old child in the hospital.

David Ervine of the Progressive Unionist party, an organization linked to the paramilitary Ulster Volunteer Force, said that the two events were "potentially the beginning of a spiral" of sectarian violence. A British government spokesman condemned violence from both sides.

London, Sunday 22. The Dunblane charity song "Knockin' on Heaven's Door" has been nudged out of the coveted Christmas No. 1 spot in the singles charts by the Spice Girls' "2 Become 1". The Dunblane song, which was recorded by the children at Abbey Road studios (above), sold 130,000 in its first week. The release date of the Spice Girls single was pushed back a week to avoid clashing with it.

Serb protestors face violence

Pro- and anti-government Serbs confront one another on the streets of Belgrade.

Slobodan Milosevic, the president of Serbia, today deployed thousands of riot police in the Serbian capital, Belgrade, in a desperate effort to halt mass protests that are threatening to destabilise his government.

Daily protests began over a month ago, when opposition victories in municipal elections were declared invalid. On Christmas Eve, police and government supporters attacked protestors. One man is reported to have died of injuries he received.

Zoran Djindjic, an opposition leader, told protestors: "We will always manage to last one day longer than Milosevic. They cannot keep 20,000 police in Belgrade every day, but we can hold out for six months."

LIMA, PERU, SUNDAY 22

Peruvian guerrillas release 225 hostages

Hostages after their release from the besieged Japanese ambassador's residence in Lima.

The guerrillas holding hundreds of hostages at the Japanese ambassador's residence in Lima released two thirds of their captives today. Observers say the guerrillas, members of the leftist Tupac Amaru group, have settled in for a long siege with the remaining 140 hostages. The revolutionaries are demanding the release of 300 political prisoners, but Peru's president, Alberto Fujimori, is adamant in his refusal to negotiate with the rebels.

LONDON, THURSDAY 26

Charges of ballot-rigging as Major wins poll

The Labour party has denounced the result of a phone-in poll for BBC radio's *Today* programme that chose Prime Minister John Major as the Personality of the Year. Labour claimed that the vote was clearly rigged. The accusation came after the BBC revealed that it had disqualified 4,000 votes for Mr. Major, as they were repeat calls from the same telephone number.

The BBC is considering dropping the annual poll, which has been discredited by political manoeuvring. Tony Blair, the opposition leader, had been banned from the poll before Christmas because of evidence that a Labour party activist was trying to influence voting in his favour.

Lisa Potts, the Wolverhampton nursery teacher who protected her pupils from a machete attack in July, came second in the poll.

London, Monday 23. Ronnie Scott, British jazz musician and founder of the famous music club in Soho that bears his name, was found dead at his Chelsea home today, aged 69.

No longer with us

January 8, François Mitterrand
President of France from 1981 to 1995, Mitterrand was one of Europe's most influential post-war leaders. He was a socialist, but of moderate convictions.

February 2, Gene Kelly
An Irish American from Pittsburgh, Kelly was at his peak as a dancer and actor in Hollywood musicals of the 1940s and 1950s, such as *Singin' in the Rain*.

February 14, Bob Paisley
As manager of Liverpool football club, Paisley won 13 major trophies in nine years, including six league championships.

February 27, Pat Smythe
The most successful woman showjumper of all time, Smythe won an Olympic bronze medal in 1956.

March 6, Douglas Jay
Lord Jay was a Labour MP for 37 years, and President of the Board of Trade from 1964 to 1967. He was an ardent opponent of British membership of the EU.

March 6, Simon Cadell
A talented stage actor, Cadell was known to a wider public chiefly for his role in the television series *Hi-de-Hi*.

March 9, George Burns
American comedian Burns is best remembered for his double act with his wife, Gracie Allen, in the 1950s.

May 20, Jon Pertwee
In the 1970s, Pertwee starred as the eponymous hero of the BBC TV science fiction series *Dr Who*. He also played *Worzel Gummidge* on children's TV.

May 31, Timothy Leary
Once a psychologist at Harvard, Leary gained international renown in the 1960s as an advocate of psychedelic drugs.

June 15, Ella Fitzgerald
Jazz singer Fitzgerald was at her peak in the 1940s and 1950s. She perfected the style of wordless singing known as "scat".

June 23, Ray Lindwall
Australian cricketer Lindwall was one of the greatest fast bowlers in the history of the game. He took 228 Test wickets.

June 23, Andreas Papandreou
Greek socialist Papandreou dominated the political life of his country for almost 20 years. He was prime minister of Greece from 1981–89 and 1993–96.

July 30, Claudette Colbert
Actress Colbert was one of the greatest Hollywood stars of the 1930s. Her most memorable movie performance was in Frank Capra's *It Happened One Night*.

August 6, Ossie Clark
Fashion designer Clark was one of the trendiest figures at the heart of the "swinging London" of the 1960s.

August 9, Sir Frank Whittle
An officer in the Royal Air Force, Whittle invented the first jet engine, which was tested in 1937.

September 17, Spiro Agnew
US vice president under Richard Nixon, Spiro Agnew was forced to resign over allegations of corruption at the time of the Watergate scandal in 1973.

September 22, Dorothy Lamour
Film actress Lamour starred with Bing Crosby and Bob Hope in the "Road" movies of the 1940s and 1950s.

September 28, Leslie Crowther
TV comedian Crowther first came to prominence in the BBC's children's programme *Crackerjack*. He later became a much-loved game-show host.

October 13, Beryl Reid
A versatile actress, Reid had her greatest successes in *The Killing of Sister George* and the TV series *Smiley's People*.

October 31, Marcel Carné
One of the great French film makers before the Second World War, Carné is best remembered for his masterpiece, *Les Enfants du Paradis*.

November 6, Tommy Lawton
An all-time great in football, Lawton played for England and Everton in the 1930s and 1940s and was renowned for his goal-scoring and heading abilities.

November 10, Marjorie Proops
The famous agony aunt of the *Daily Mirror*, Proops is said to have heard from 3 per cent of the population during her decades with the newspaper.

November 27, Michael Bentine
Comedian Bentine was a founder member of BBC radio's *The Goon Show* in the 1950s and creator of the 1960s television series *It's a Square World*.

December 11, Willie Rushton
A satirist, comedian and cartoonist, Rushton was a regular performer on BBC Radio's long-running series *I'm Sorry I Haven't A Clue*.

December 16, Laurens van der Post
A South African explorer and writer, Sir Laurens advocated a spiritual philosophy. He has been described as Prince Charles's mentor or spiritual guide.

December 19, Marcello Mastroianni
Handsome Italian actor Mastroianni starred in more than 130 movies, including *Divorce Italian Style* and Federico Fellini's classic *La Dolce Vita*.

December 20, Carl Sagan
Sagan brought physics and astronomy to a wide public through books and television. He believed in the existence of intelligent life elsewhere in the universe.

Spiro Agnew, September 17

Claudette Colbert, July 30

Dorothy Lamour, September 22

Ella Fitzgerald, June 15

Ossie Clark, August 6

ob Paisley, February 14

Gene Kelly, February 2

George Burns, March 9

Timothy Leary, May 31

Beryl Reid, October 13

President François Mitterrand, January 8

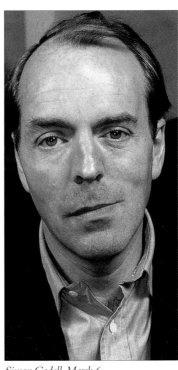

Simon Cadell, March 6

Index

117

Picture credits